GOOGLE PIXEL USER GUIDE

The Complete User Manual for Beginners and seniors to Master the New Google Pixel 7A, 7, And 7 pro with Tips and Tricks

BY

JOE K. RICHARD

Copyright © 2023 JOE K. RICHARD

All rights reserved. No part of this book shall be reproduced, stored in a retrieval system, or transmitted by any means, electronic, mechanical, photocopying, recording, or otherwise, without written permission from the publisher. Although every precaution has been taken in the preparation of this book, the publisher and author assume no responsibility for errors or omissions. Nor is any liability assumed for damages resulting from the use of the information contained herein.

LEGAL NOTICE

This book is copyright protected and is only for personal use. This book should not be amended or distributed, sold, quoted, or paraphrased without the consent of the author or publisher

Contents

INTRODUCTION 1
CHAPTER ONE 2
GET TO KNOW YOUR GOOGLE PIXEL 7A 2
    SPECIFICATIONS FOR THE GOOGLE PIXEL 7A 4
CHAPTER TWO 6
FEATURES OF GOOGLE PIXEL 7A 6
    DESIGN 6
    CAMERAS 8
    DISPLAY AND PERFORMANCE 10
    SOFTWARE 12
    HARDWARE 13
    COLORS 16
    CHARCOAL PIXEL 7A 17
    PIXEL 7A IN SNOW 19
    PIXEL 7A IN SEA 20
    PIXEL 7A IN CORAL 21
    PRICE AND AVAILABILITY 22
CHAPTER THREE 23
DIFFERENCE BETWEEN THE GOOGLE PIXEL 7 PRO, PIXEL 7, AND PIXEL 7A 23
    DESIGN 25
    DISPLAY 27
    HARDWARE AND SPECS 28
    CAMERA 29

GOOGLE PIXEL 7A VS 6A 32
GOOGLE PIXEL 7A VS PIXEL 6A: DESIGN 33
GOOGLE PIXEL 7A VS PIXEL 6A: DISPLAY 34
CAMERA 36
HARDWARE 38
STORAGE AND PERFORMANCE 39
BATTERY 40
QUALITY OF AUDIO AND HAPTICS 40
GOOGLE PIXEL 7A VS PIXEL 6A: SOFTWARE .. 41

CHAPTER FOUR 43
HOW TO SET UP YOUR GOOGLE PIXEL 7A 43
HOW TO SET UP THE GOOGLE PIXEL 7A FACE UNLOCK 46
HOW TO TURN ON THE PIXEL 7A 90HZ SCREEN 51

CHAPTER FIVE 53
BASIC SETTINGS TO CHANGE AS SOON AS YOU UNBOX YOUR NEW PIXEL 7A 53
HOW TO SEND A TEXT TO A FRIEND QUICKLY BY USING VOICE TYPING 53
UTILIZE THE QUICK TAP GESTURE TO CAPTURE SCREENSHOTS 54
USE DIGITAL WELL-BEING TO GET BETTER AT USING YOUR PHONE 54
USE A SHORTCUT TO LAUNCH THE CAMERA RIGHT AWAY. 56

CHECK THE PERCENTAGE OF BATTERY LIFE IN THE STATUS BAR. 57

HOW TO MAKE PIXEL 7A'S TOUCH SENSITIVE 57

HOW TO CHANGE SCREEN RESOLUTION 58

GESTURE-ACTIVATED FLASHLIGHT ON/OFF 59

HOW TO ACTIVATE NOW PLAYING 60

SET UP RULES TO AUTOMATE YOUR DEVICE 60

USE LIVE TRANSLATION ON THE PHONE, IN VIDEOS, AND OTHER 61

HOW TO TURN ON "ONE-HAND MODE" 62

HOW TO CHANGE YOUR QUICK SETTINGS SO THAT SHORTCUTS ARE EASY TO ACCESS 63

CONFIGURE SAFETY FEATURES LIKE HEADS-UP AND CRASH DETECTION 63

TURN ON THE ADAPTIVE ALERT VIBRATION MODE 64

CHANGE BETWEEN THE FRONT AND BACK CAMERAS WITH A SIMPLE TWIST 65

MAKE THE MOST OF GOOGLE'S PHOTOGRAPHY AND CAMERA TOOLS. 65

HOW TO SET UP GRID LINES 67

HOW TO GET RID OF AN ALARM OR PHONE CALL WITHOUT SAYING "HEY GOOGLE" 67

ADD A GOOGLE ACCOUNT THAT ALREADY EXISTS 68

    TRANSFER PHOTOS OR VIDEOS TO YOUR
COMPUTER 69

    METHODS FOR TRANSFERRING DATA FROM
PIXEL TO PIXEL 70

CHAPTER SIX 73

CAMERA 73

    FEATURES OF GOOGLE PIXEL 7A CAMERAS .. 73

    GOOGLE PIXEL 7A CAMERAS SHOOTOUT 76

    VERY SOLID HDR PERFORMANCE 76

    EXCELLENT NIGHTTIME AND LOW-LIGHT
PHOTOGRAPHY 77

    ENHANCED NIGHT SIGHT 79

    LONG EXPOSURE 79

    HIGH RES ZOOM 79

    NEW CAMERA FOR SELFIES 80

    GOOGLE PIXEL 7A CAMERA VS GOOGLE PIXEL
7 CAMERA 81

    PIXEL 7 VS PIXEL 7A: CAMERA SPECS 81

    PIXEL 7 VS PIXEL 7A: MAIN CAMERA 82

CHAPTER SEVEN 87

MESSAGES 87

    HOW TO USE GOOGLE PIXEL PHONES' AUDIO
MESSAGE TRANSCRIPTION FEATURE 87

    HOW TO SEND A MESSAGE 89

    HOW TO QUICKLY DELETE SMS ON A PIXEL
PHONE 89

- HOW TO GET DELETED TEXTS BACK ON A GOOGLE PIXEL PHONE 90
- HOW TO USE GOOGLE PIXEL'S BUILT-IN BACKUP TO GET BACK DELETED TEXTS 91
- HOW TO RECOVER DELETED SMS ON GOOGLE PIXEL WITHOUT BACKUP USING COOLMUSTER ANDROID SMS + CONTACTS RECOVERY 91

CHAPTER EIGHT 94

PHOTOS 94
- USE PHOTO UNBLUR TO FIX SHOTS THAT ARE BLURRY 94
- USE A MAGIC ERASER TO GET RID OF DISTRACTIONS 96
- USE PORTRAIT BLUR TO MAKE YOUR SUBJECT STAND OUT 97
- USE PORTRAIT LIGHT TO IMPROVE THE LIGHT ON FACES 97
- SKY IDEAS CAN CHANGE THE MOOD AND TONE OF YOUR SUNSET PHOTOS. 97
- USE THE COLLAGE TOOL TO CREATE THINGS THAT CAN BE SHARED. 98
- HOW TO CHANGE THE COLOR OF THE SKY IN GOOGLE PHOTOS 98

CHAPTER NINE 100

TRANSFER OF DATA 100

5 METHODS FOR TRANSFERRING DATA FROM ONE PIXEL TO ANOTHER 101

USE THE GOOGLE DATA TRANSFER TOOL APP 101

USE AIRDROID PERSONAL 102

USE BLUETOOTH 104

UTILIZE GOOGLE DRIVE 105

USE A COMPUTER 106

CHAPTER TEN 109

BACK UP YOUR GOOGLE PIXEL PHONE AND RESTORE IT 109

HOW TO BACK UP AND RESTORE GOOGLE PIXEL ON PC WITH COOLMUSTER ANDROID BACKUP MANAGER 110

HOW TO USE THE PHONE BACKUP & RESET FEATURE TO BACK UP AND RESTORE YOUR GOOGLE PIXEL 112

HOW TO USE THE GOOGLE DRIVE APP TO BACK UP AND RESTORE A GOOGLE PIXEL ... 114

CHAPTER ELEVEN 116

HOW TO SET UP AND USE GOOGLE PIXEL PHONES' PERSONAL SAFETY APP 116

HOW TO SET UP THE PERSONAL SAFETY APP AND RUNNING 116

HOW TO TURN ON THE EMERGENCY SOS NOTIFICATION 118

- HOW TO USE THE CAR CRASH DETECTION SYSTEM 118
- CHECK FOR SAFETY AND HOW TO USE IT 119
- HOW TO TURN ON IN AN EMERGENCY SHARING 120

CHAPTER TWELVE 121

MUSIC 121
- HOW TO GET SONG INFO AUTOMATICALLY 121
- UTILIZE MUSIC SEARCH TO ACCESS ADDITIONAL SONGS. 122
- FIND THE MUSIC YOU'VE JUST HEARD 123
- FAVORITE MUSIC YOU'VE EVER HEARD 123
- MODIFY WHERE NOTIFICATIONS ARE DISPLAYED 124
- GOOGLE PIXEL'S NOW PLAYING 124
- HOW TO INSTALL AMBIENT MUSIC MOD 126

CHAPTER THIRTEEN 130

HOW TO USE GOOGLE PIXEL PHONES' LIVE CAPTION FEATURE 130
- HOW TO ACTIVATE OR DEACTIVATE LIVE CAPTION 130
- HOW TO USE LIVE CAPTION 132
- MANAGING LIVE CAPTION SETTINGS 132
- YOU CAN TYPE RESPONSES BY USING A LIVE CAPTION 133

CHAPTER FOURTEEN 134

- GOOGLE ASSISTANT SCREEN CALLS 134
  - HOW TO SET UP SCREEN CALLING ON YOUR GOOGLE PIXEL 134
  - HOW TO GET THE TRANSCRIPTS OF YOUR SCREENED CALLS OR PRESERVE THE RECORDINGS 136
  - HOW TO MODIFY THE ASSISTANT VOICE FOR SCREENED CALLS 137
  - CLEAR CALLING ON PIXEL 7A 137
  - HOW TO TURN CLEAR CALLING ON OR OFF 138
- CHAPTER FIFTEEN 140
- RECOVER DELETED CONTACTS ON GOOGLE PIXEL 140
  - HOW CAN TO RECOVER DELETED CONTACTS WITHOUT BACKUP VIA COOLMUSTER ANDROID SMS + CONTACTS RECOVERY 143
  - HOW TO GET DELETED CONTACTS BACK FROM GOOGLE BACKUP 145
- CHAPTER SIXTEEN 146
- DRIVING MODE ON YOUR GOOGLE PIXEL 7A .. 146
  - HOW TO SET UP A DRIVING RULE 147
  - HOW TO ENABLE DO NOT DISTURB ON PIXEL 7A 147
  - DO NOT DISTURB MODE COULD BE HELPFUL IN MANY SITUATIONS 149
- CHAPTER SEVENTEEN 151

HOW TO SET THE PIXEL 7A TO USE 10-BIT COLOR FOR VIDEOS 151

    HOW TO UTILIZE THE GOOGLE PIXEL'S MAGIC ERASER 152

CHAPTER EIGHTEEN 155

GOOGLE ASSISTANT'S HOLD FOR ME FEATURE 155

    WHAT IS THE HOLD FOR ME FEATURE IN GOOGLE ASSISTANT, AND HOW DOES IT WORK? 155

    HOW TO TURN ON THE FUNCTION AND USE IT 156

    DURING A CALL, PUT ME ON HOLD. 156

CHAPTER NINETEEN 157

HOW TO RESET YOUR GOOGLE PIXEL 7A 157

    BASIC RESTART 159

    FACTORY RESET 159

    FORCE RESTART 159

TWENTY 161

TIPS AND TRICKS 161

    OPEN THE CAMERA QUICKLY 161

    GET TO GOOGLE PAY QUICKLY FROM THE LOCK SCREEN 161

    MULTILINGUAL KEYBOARD 162

    TURN ON THE QUICK TAP 162

    CHANGE THE SIZE OF THE KEYBOARD 163

SIGN UP TWICE WITH YOUR FINGERS 163
TURN OFF YOUR MIC OR CAMERA QUICKLY 164
ADD A RAW SWITCH TO THE CAMERA 164
STOP USING THE GOOGLE DISCOVER PAGE 165
AUTOMATICALLY FIND SONGS 165
CONCLUSION 167
INDEX 168

INTRODUCTION

The Google Pixel 7a is Google's latest entry-level Android smartphone. Announced at this year's I/O conference, the 7a boasts an impressive amount of technology and features for the money. In particular, it receives the most recent processor and security features from Google, in addition to wireless charging, a better display, and a significantly updated main camera. The Pixel 7a is an excellent phone. It looks good, has great specs, a good camera system, and costs only $499, which is pretty easy on the pocket.

CHAPTER ONE

GET TO KNOW YOUR GOOGLE PIXEL 7A

The Google Pixel 7A has several interesting features. It has a **6.1-inch OLED display** with a full-**HD+ resolution** and a **90Hz refresh rate.** This is a first for the Pixel A-line, which had always used the standard **60Hz refresh rate.** Corning's Gorilla Glass 3 protects the screen, and **HDR** makes it easier to see what's on the screen.

Under the hood, Google put its latest Tensor **G2 SoC,** which is the same chip found in the high-end Pixel 7 and Pixel 7 Pro smartphones. With the Titan M2 security co-processor and **8GB of LPDDR5 RAM and 128GB of UFS 3.1 storage,** this processor is very powerful.

The Pixel 7A has a main camera with **64 megapixels** and optical image stabilization (OIS). It also has an improved ultra-wide-angle camera with **13 megapixels.** There is a 13MP camera on the front for taking pictures and video chatting.

The Pixel 7A has a **4,385mAh battery,** which is smaller than the cell in the Pixel 6A. Also, there is no charger included with the phone. But Google has added something big to the Pixel 7A: **wireless charge,** which is a first for the A-series.

Pros of the Google Pixel 7A

- Quality 6.1-inch OLED screen with a rotation rate of 90Hz
- The latest Tensor G2 SoC chip has 8GB LPDDR5 RAM and 128GBUFS 3.1 storage.
- Improvements to the camera, including a 64-megapixel main camera with OIS
- Support for wireless charging using the Qi standard, which is widely used.

Cons

- Compared to its predecessor, the Pixel 6A, it has a smaller battery size.
- The box that came with it does not indicate a charger.

SPECIFICATIONS FOR THE GOOGLE PIXEL 7A

- Screen: 6.1in 90Hz FHD+ OLED (429ppi)
- Processor: Google Tensor G2
- RAM: 8GB
- Storage: 128GB
- Operating system: Android 13
- Camera: 64 MP + 13 MP for ultra-wide, 13 MP for selfie
- Connectivity: 5G, eSIM, WiFi 6E, NFC, Bluetooth 5.3, and GNSS connect.
- Dimensions: 152.4 x 72.9 x 9mm
- Weight: 193g
- Google Tensor G2 chipset
- 4385mAh
- Fast charging with 18W,
- wireless charging with 7.5W
- Bluetooth 5.3

Here's what your new Pixel 7a phone comes with:

- Pixel phone
- SIM tool
- Quick Switch Adapter
- A 1-m USB 2.0 to USB C cable

- Support Card

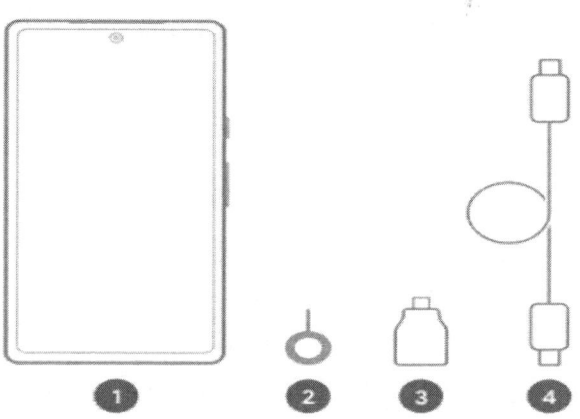

CHAPTER TWO

FEATURES OF GOOGLE PIXEL 7A

DESIGN

The Pixel 7a only features a few minor differences from the original. However, the corners are made of metal and the back is made of high-gloss plastic that, until touched, appears to be glass. The aluminum frame of the Pixel 7a is the same color as the device you select, unlike the Pixel 6a's frame, which was black since it was polished. My Snow review device's frame is silver.

Because the camera bar of the Pixel 6a was similarly made of plastic, you could tell that it was the less expensive model. But the Pixel 7a now has a metal camera bar, just like the Pixel 7, but its a little thinner (possibly because the sensors are smaller).

The Pixel 7a is also a little bit bigger and wider than the Pixel 6a, but you won't be able to tell unless you put them side by side. The Pixel 7a is 72.9mm by 152.4mm by 9.0mm, while the Pixel 6a is 71.8mm by 152.2mm by 8.9mm. The Pixel 7a weighs 193 grams, which is a bit more than the Pixel 7's 178 grams. Even though the Pixel 7a is slightly smaller than the Pixel 7, it still has the same 6.1-inch screen as the Pixel 7. This makes it the smallest of the Pixel 7 phones.

Because the Pixel 7a is a little bit smaller than the Pixel 7, it's easier to hold. But as someone who usually likes smaller phones, I wish the Pixel 7a was the same size as its predecessor, which was easier for me to hold easily. But overall, the Pixel 7a looks pretty much the same as other Pixel phones. Instead of Gorilla Glass Victus on the back, it has high-gloss plastic instead.

Google says that the Pixel 7a is one of the most durable devices in the Pixel A line so far. It has an IP67 grade, which means that it can handle dust and water without any problems. Corning Gorilla Glass 3 is also used for the front screen, making it hard to scratch.

CAMERAS

Even though the Pixel 7a is the least expensive of the Pixel 7 phones, Google gave it a camera that is just as good as that of the Pixel 7 and Pixel 7 Pro.

The Pixel 7a has a main camera with 64MP and a wide-angle camera with 13MP. In comparison, both the Pixel 7 and Pixel 7 Pro have a main camera with 50MP and a wide-angle camera with 12MP. But Google says that the Pixel 7a's sensor is not as big as the ones on the Pixel 7 and 7 Pro, even though it has more megapixels than its brothers. The 64MP camera is nothing to scoff at. It takes shots that are very clear and detailed without looking too processed. The colors are also bright and clear, but not too bright like on most Samsung phones or too harsh like on my iPhone 14 Pro when it's bright outside.

Even when it was cloudy and dark outside, the Pixel 7a did a good job taking pictures, and the pictures turned out great despite the weather. And again, the Pixel 7a's Tensor G2 chip makes it very quick to take a picture, so I can get good shots even when my baby is on the move.

The selfie camera on the Pixel 7a is also a big improvement over the 8MP camera on its predecessor and the 10.8MP camera on the Pixel 7 base model. On the Pixel 7a, the front-facing camera is 13MP. I think the Pixel 7a gets great selfies that are clear and have just the right amount of blur in the background when taken in Portrait mode. This is also true for Portrait photos taken with the back camera.

DISPLAY AND PERFORMANCE

The Pixel 7a has the same 6.1-inch screen size as the Pixel 6a. It also has a Full HD OLED screen with a size of 1080 x 2400, a ratio of 20:9, and Corning Gorilla Glass 3 to protect it. But Google made a few small changes that made the Pixel 7a a bit better.

In the past, Pixel A-series phones had a frame rate of 60Hz, which was common for cheap phones at the time. But the new Pixel 7a has a smoother 90Hz adjustable refresh rate, which is called "Smooth Display." It's the same setting as the normal Pixel 7, which also has a frame rate of 90Hz.

With a higher refresh rate, you can expect smoother scrolling, animations, and better images when you play games. But Smooth Display is turned off by default, so you have to turn it on yourself. This is possible because the Pixel 7a has a short battery life (a higher refresh rate makes battery life shorter), which we'll talk about in a moment.

Google put the newer Tensor G2 chip inside, which is better than the Pixel 6a's first-generation Tensor chip. You also have 8GB of RAM, which is more than the 6a's 6GB, and again, 128GB is the only storage choice.

During my testing with the Pixel 7a, I found that it works well for my everyday jobs. This includes using an app to share a ton of pictures of my toddler daughter with family, checking my email and messages on Microsoft Teams, scrolling endlessly through Instagram and Facebook, checking Mastodon, watching streaming videos and YouTube, reading the news, and playing a few light, casual games. The Pixel 7a works well at all of these things and doesn't miss a beat.

I'm also surprised by how quickly the cameras can take a picture. I've taken a lot of photos with the Pixel 7a of my toddler. Tensor G2 is a big part of why the Pixel 7a can take pictures so quickly.

SOFTWARE

Like the Pixel 7 and Pixel 7 Pro, the Pixel 7a comes with Android 13 out of the box. The Pixel 7a will also receive OS upgrades for three years and security patches for five years, just like the other Pixel 7 variants.

Android 13 is pretty grown up at this point, while Android 14 is just starting to show itself. Android 13 is the first version of Android I've spent a lot of time with, and I loved it on the

Pixel 7a. This is the "pure" form of Android, which means that the manufacturer didn't add any skins to it.

Android 13 is simple and clean, with no special forks. A lot of the AI features on the Pixel 7a are also very appealing thanks to Google's Tensor chip. This is a big reason to think about getting the Pixel 7a, or any Pixel, for that matter. For example, Magic Eraser works great, and you can use Google Assistant to hold your place in line and more on your phone.

Overall, the Pixel 7a's software works well because Google improved its specs to make it run faster. It's easy to use and works quickly. You can't go wrong with the Pixel 7a if you like the stock Android experience.

HARDWARE

The Pixel 7a has a frame made of metal, a back made of plastic, and a screen made of Gorilla Glass 3. The camera bar is made of the same metal as the frame. It has stereo microphones, one on the bottom edge and the other on the top that can also be used as an earpiece. A USB-C port lets you charge your device and connect it to other things.

The Pixel 7a has the Google Tensor G2 system-on-chip, 8 GB of RAM, and 128 GB of UFS 3.1 storage that can't be expanded.

The Pixel 7a has a battery that can hold 4385 mAh and can be charged quickly at up to 18 W. It can also be charged wirelessly. It has a water safety level of IP67.

The Pixel 7a has a 6.1-inch, 1080p OLED screen that supports HDR and has a frame rate of 90 Hz. The screen has a 20:9 aspect ratio and a hole for the front-facing camera in the top center.

On the back of the Pixel 7a are two cameras. In contrast to the ultrawide 120° f/2.2 lens, which has a 13-megapixel sensor, the wide 26 mm f/1.9 lens sports a 64-megapixel sensor. The 13-megapixel sensor on the front-facing camera is also present. 4K video can be captured at either 30 or 60 frames per second.

Diagram of the Google Pixel 7A

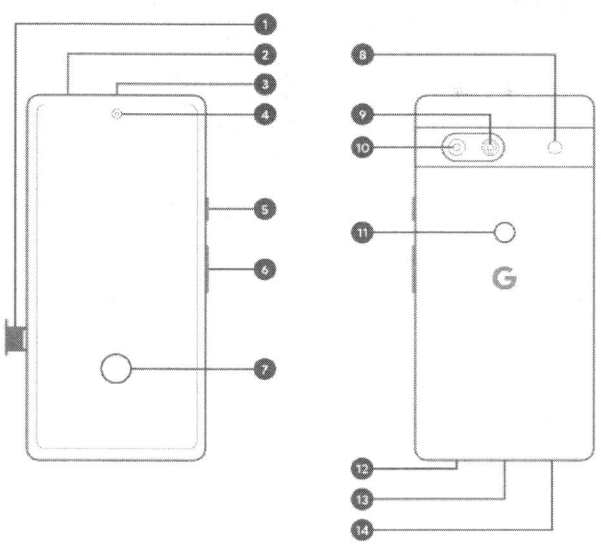

- SIM card tray
- Top Microphone
- Top speaker
- Front-facing camera
- Power button
- Volume up/down
- Fingerprint sensor
- LED flash
- Rear-facing camera: UltraWide lens
- Rear-facing camera: Wide lens
- NFC
- Bottom speaker
- USB-C port
- Bottom microphone

COLORS

The Pixel 7a can be bought in four different colors: charcoal, snow, sea, and coral. Unlike the Pixel 6a from the year before, the camera bar on the Pixel 7a doesn't come in only black. Instead, it is made to fit the color of each device, though the color of the camera bar will be slightly different from the main color of the phone. The body and camera bar of the Pixel 7a feature a brushed metal appearance, while the back side has a glossy finish. Some people might have liked the difference between last year's models better, but the Pixel 7a looks whole and consistent because the body and camera bar is the same color. So, the Charcoal and Snow color options are almost the same as the Charcoal and Chalk options on the Pixel 6a. The color-matched camera bar does change the way the phone looks. It gives the Charcoal phone a space gray tint like the iPhone and gives the Snow phone a silver tint. Sea and Coral are where the fun starts, though. The sea is a bright light blue, and Coral is a bright color that looks like a mix of pink and orange. Both colors feel like summer and are great if you want your new phone to make a statement. But the Pixel 7a in Coral is only sold at the Google Store, so you'll have to go there to get it.

Google chose the colors for the Pixel 7a so that they were the best of both worlds. If you like simple colors, you might like Charcoal and Snow because they are mostly black and white. But, unlike the Pixel 7 and Pixel 7 Pro, the Pixel 7a also comes in the Sea and Coral colors, which are much lighter. The Pixel 7a is a lot like the Pixel 7, which is one of the best Android phones you can buy. It's a good choice at a fair price, and it comes in great colors and has a lot of great features.

CHARCOAL PIXEL 7A

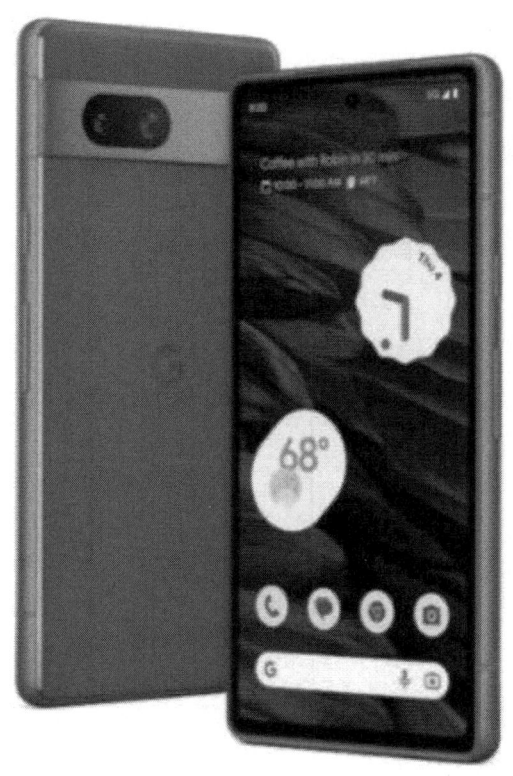

Charcoal is the darkest color for the Pixel 7a. Charcoal is a nice, solid, classy gray color that is not quite black.

Because it's a dark, muted color, the Pixel 7a Charcoal can go with any style and look good in both business and casual settings. Charcoal is also a lot less noticeable than other color options, so it's a great choice if you want to use your phone without drawing too much attention to it.

PIXEL 7A IN SNOW

The Pixel 7a in Snow is a great choice for people who want a lighter color that, like the Charcoal version, goes with almost everything.

The Pixel 7a's color is snow, which is white. It's a nice, bright highlight color that's just as stylish as the darker Charcoal. The elegant look is completed by the silver camera bar and metal frame, which match the classic white design of the back.

PIXEL 7A IN SEA

The first two colors are pretty typical for the Pixel A-line, but the light blue Sea color stands out. The sea is the perfect color for summer and a great choice for anyone who wants to add some color to their style.

The sea is a beautiful shade of blue, but its color isn't very bright. This is a first for Google since most of the Pixel 7 and Pixel 7 Pro colors are green.

PIXEL 7A IN CORAL

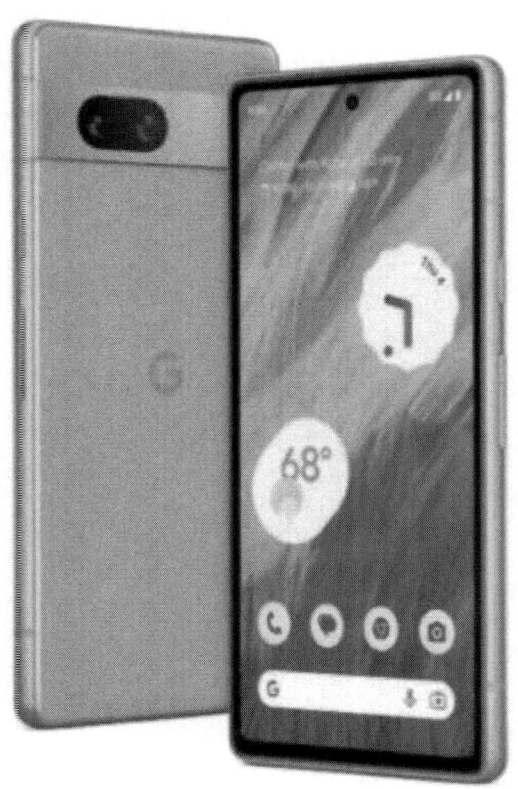

Coral is the Pixel 7a color that stands out the most. But you probably won't see many of them out and about because they're only sold at Google retail shops and on the Google Store website.

PRICE AND AVAILABILITY

The Pixel 7a from Google can be bought right now for $499. You can buy it from Google directly, from stores like Amazon and Best Buy, or from a wireless service. The Pixel 7a is available in four colors: Charcoal, Snow, Sea, and Coral, which is only sold at the Google Store.

The Pixel 7a's price puts it in an odd spot and makes it hard to suggest, especially since the Pixel 6a is still being sold for $349, which is a new low.

The Pixel 6a is the best Pixel phone for the least amount of money, and it's still a great phone. But the Pixel 7a is better if you want more megapixels, a faster refresh rate, and a wireless charge.

CHAPTER THREE

DIFFERENCE BETWEEN THE GOOGLE PIXEL 7 PRO, PIXEL 7, AND PIXEL 7A

Google announced the Pixel 7 Pro and the Pixel 7 in October 2022. The Pixel 7a, a mid-range phone, was announced at Google I/O on May 10, 2023.

The Pixel 7 Pro and Pixel 7 devices replace the excellent Pixel 6 Pro and Pixel 6, with updated technology, a better design, and some exciting new features. The Pixel 7a replaces the excellent Pixel 6a.

If you want to know how the Pixel 7a compares to the Pixel 7 Pro and the Pixel 7, don't worry, I've got you covered. Here is a comparison of the Pixel 7 Pro, the Pixel 7, and the Pixel 7a to help you decide which Pixel phone is right for you.

AT GLANCE

Google Pixel 7 Pro

Google Pixel 7

Google Pixel 7a

GOOGLE PIXEL 7 PRO

The Pixel 7 Pro costs more than the Pixel 7, but it has an extra camera sensor, a bigger battery, more memory, and a beautiful curved screen. If you have the money, you should get the Pro model. It's a great tool that has a lot to love.

GOOGLE PIXEL 7

The Pixel 7 is a great phone. The Pixel 7 Pro has some extra features, but the Pixel 7 is still a great phone with a good camera, long battery life, and a lot of power. But you should think about getting the Pixel 7a.

GOOGLE PIXEL 7A

Google's new mid-range phone is the Pixel 7a. It comes after the Pixel 6a and sits between the Pixel 7 and the Pixel 7 Pro. It's a great device that has a lot of the same features as the Pixel 7, but the camera is set up differently and is still great.

DESIGN

Both the Pixel 7 Pro and Pixel 7 have a camera housing on the back that runs the width of the device, just like the Pixel 6 and Pixel 6 Pro. Since the Pixel 6 and 6 Pro, the style has been tweaked, but it's still mostly the same, and the Pixel 7a is the same.

Both the Pixel 7 Pro and Pixel 7 have a luxurious finish, and both are resistant to water and dust (IP68). The Pixel 7 Pro has a polished aluminum frame, while the Pixel 7 has a smooth aluminum frame. Both phones have Corning Gorilla Glass Victus cover glass and edgeless Corning Gorilla Glass Victus backs. The Pixel 7a is based on the Pixel 7, but like the Pixel 6a, it has a slightly lower IP grade of IP67.

The Pixel 7 Pro is bigger and heavier than the Pixel 7 and Pixel 7 Pro. It's also bigger and heavier than the Pixel 7a, which is the smallest device in the line. Both the Pixel 7 Pro and Pixel 7 come in white (Snow) and black (Obsidian), but the third color is different. The Pixel 7 is available in Lemongrass, while the 7 Pro comes in Hazel. The Pixel 7a, on the other hand, comes in four colors: Charcoal, Snow, Sea, and Coral. The first two are black and white, while the third is blue. The only way to get Coral is through the Google Store. The Pixel 7 and 7 Pro, as well as the Pixel 7a, don't have a two-tone back like the Pixel 6 Pro and Pixel 6.

On the front, both the Pixel 7 Pro and the Pixel 7 have a hole-punch camera in the middle of the top of their screens. The Pixel 7 Pro's display is slightly curved, while the Pixel 7's is flat. The Pixel 7a has a flat-screen like the Pixel 7, but it also has a camera hole in the middle of the top. Both the Pixel 7 and 7 Pro have fingerprint readers under the screen, which the Pixel 7a also has, and they all have Face Unlock, which is new to the Pixel "A" line.

DISPLAY

The Google Pixel 7 Pro has a 6.7-inch LTPO OLED screen that can be refreshed up to 120 times per second. It has a Quad HD+ screen (3120 x 1440), which gives it the same pixel density as the Pixel 6 Pro (512ppi).

The Pixel 7 has a 6.3-inch OLED screen that is not LTPO but is still an OLED panel. It has a resolution of 2400 x 1080, which gives it a pixel density of 416ppi, and a frame rate of 90Hz.

The Pixel 7a, on the other hand, has an OLED screen that is 6.1 inches and, like the Pixel 7, is not LTPO. It has a Full HD+ resolution of 2400 x 1080, giving it a pixel density of 431ppi, and a refresh rate of 90Hz, which is the same as the Pixel 7. This means that the Pixel 7 Pro has a sharper screen than the Pixel

7 and Pixel 7a. It should also move more smoothly, but you might not notice unless you compare it to the Pixel 7 or Pixel 7a side by side.

As was already mentioned, the Pixel 7 Pro has a little curved screen, while the Pixel 7 and Pixel 7a equally have flat screens. However, all three Pixel 7 models have HDR support.

HARDWARE AND SPECS

The Pixel 7 Pro and Pixel 7 both use the Google Tensor G2 chip, which is the next version of the Google Tensor chip. The Pixel 7a also uses this processor. The chip gives photos, videos, protection, and speech recognition more power. The Pixel 7 Pro, Pixel 7, and Pixel 7a all have the Titan M2 security chip, and all three can get security patches for five years.

The Pixel 7 Pro has 12GB of RAM, while the Pixel 7 and Pixel 7a both have 8GB. This puts the 7 and 7a closer to the Pixel 7 Pro than the Pro is to the 7 and 7a. On the Pixel 7, you can choose between 128GB and 256GB of storage. On the Pixel 7 Pro, you can also get 512GB of storage. The Pixel 7a, on the other hand, only comes with 128GB of storage. The Pixel 7 and

7 Pro don't work with microSD cards to add more storage, and the Pixel 7a doesn't either.

The Pixel 7 Pro has a 5000mAh battery, just like the Pixel 6 Pro did. The Pixel 7, on the other hand, has a 4355mAh cell. Both can charge up to 50% in 30 minutes with fast charging, and they both have wireless charging and Battery Share, which is also called reverse wireless charging. The Pixel 7a has a 4385mAh battery, which makes it a little bit bigger than the Pixel 7, but not by much. It's also the first Pixel "a" device to have wireless charge.

CAMERA

Aside from size and a few design details, the Pixel 7 Pro and Pixel 7 have very different cameras. The Pixel 7a has even more differences in this area. On the back of the Pixel 7 Pro, there are three cameras, while the Pixel 7 only has two. The Pixel 7a also has two cameras, but it is built differently than the Pixel 7.

The Pixel 7 Pro's triple rear camera has a 48-megapixel telephoto lens (f/3.5, 0.7m) with 5x optical zoom, a 50-megapixel main sensor (f/1.85, 1.2m) with an 82-degree field of view, and a 12-megapixel super wide sensor (f/2.2, 1.25m) with a 125.8-degree field of view.

The zoom lens is absent from the Pixel 7 camera, which shares the same primary sensor and ultra-wide sensor as the Pixel 7 Pro.

A 13-megapixel ultra-wide lens and a 64-megapixel primary camera sensor are both featured on the Pixel 7a. It's important to note that just because a camera has more megapixels doesn't mean it's better. In our experience, the Pixel 7 Pro does a better job than the Pixel 7a, even though the 7a's main sensor has a lower resolution.

Motion Mode, Real Tone, Photo Unblur, and Magic Eraser are all features of the Pixel 7 Pro and Pixel 7 phones, as well as the company's great Night Sight. These features are also available on the Pixel 7a, so you get the full Pixel experience across the board. The Pixel 7 Pro has Macro Focus and a 30x high-resolution zoom, but the Pixel 7 and Pixel 7a only have an 8x high-resolution zoom and don't have the Macro Focus feature.

Both the Pixel 7 Pro and the Pixel 7 have a front-facing camera with 10.8 megapixels (f/2.2, 1.22m), which can record 4K video. The Pixel 7a has a 13-megapixel front camera, which means it has the highest quality of the three Pixel phones. However, as we said about the main camera, this doesn't mean it's the best.

Summary

The Pixel 7 Pro, Pixel 7, and Pixel 7a all have a similar look, but there are a few changes, like the back camera, size, and color. The Pixel 7 Pro has a slightly curved screen, unlike the Pixel 7 and Pixel 7a, which have flat screens. It also has a better resolution, a faster refresh rate, more RAM, more storage, and a bigger battery.

The Pixel 7 Pro, Pixel 7, and Pixel 7a all have different cameras, which is where you can see the biggest difference between them. The Pixel 7 Pro has a telephoto sensor and more camera features than the Pixel 7 and Pixel 7a, like Macro focus and a better resolution zoom.

GOOGLE PIXEL 7A VS 6A

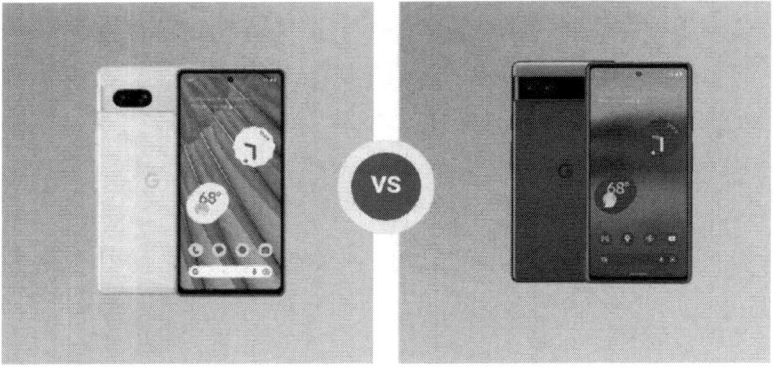

A comparison of the Google Pixel 7a and Pixel 6a shows all the changes Google made to its cheap phone this year, and there are a lot of them. Google's latest middle phone has more in common with the Pixel 7 than with its predecessor. This is because Google wants to keep making one of the best cheap phones even as competition grows.

To do this, the Pixel 7a has a new fast-refreshing screen, the ability to charge wirelessly, and a better back camera array. But adding the Tensor G2 engine, which brings the same AI-powered features as the Pixel 7, could be the biggest change. In our review of the Pixel 7a, we explain how these changes affect Google's middle phone.

Even though the Pixel 7a is the phone that comes after the Pixel 6a, it doesn't completely replace the phone. The Pixel 6a is still available, but Google has dropped the price. If you choose the Pixel 6a, you'll get a phone with the same chipset as the Pixel 6, but it will cost you much less than it did before.

Want to know how the Pixel 6a and Pixel 7a relate to each other? Here is a quick list of the most important differences:

- The processor in the Pixel 7a is faster than the processor in the Pixel 6a.
- The Pixel 7a can be charged wirelessly, while the Pixel 6a can't.
- The camera on the Pixel 7a is better than the camera on the Pixel 6a.
- The Pixel 6a costs less than half as much as the Pixel 7a.

GOOGLE PIXEL 7A VS PIXEL 6A: DESIGN

Like the Pixel 6a, the Pixel 7a has a similar appearance. There are two cameras on the back of the phone in a horizontal bar that runs across the back of the phone. Unlike Google's flagship phones, the A Series phones tend to have slightly bigger bezels around the screen, and this one is no exception.

Because the Pixel 7a is more like the Pixel 7, the camera bar is a little more polished, but the back is made of plastic instead of metal. The Pixel 7a and Pixel 6a are both 6 x 2.8 x 0.4 inches, but the Pixel 7a weighs half an ounce more than the Pixel 6a.

With the Pixel 7a, you can choose from one more color, Coral, which is only available at Google's shop. Other than that, the Pixel 7a comes in Snow, Charcoal, and Sea, which is a light blue. The Pixel 6a came in Charcoal, Chalk, and Sage.

GOOGLE PIXEL 7A VS PIXEL 6A: DISPLAY

The Pixel 7a has the same 6.1-inch OLED screen as its predecessor. The resolution of this screen is 2400 x 1080. But the Pixel 7a has a big edge over the Pixel 6a because its display has a faster refresh rate.

No matter what is on the Pixel 6a's screen, the rate is always 60Hz. But you can change a Pixel 7a setting to make the refresh rate go up to 90Hz for times when you want smoother scrolling and more realistic pictures. When turned on, the Pixel 7a display's refresh rate goes from 60Hz to 90Hz on its own.

The Pixel 7a has a better screen than the Pixel 6a, with 931 nits instead of 778 nits. Both phones capture about 111% of the sRGB color gamut in Natural mode, but we thought the colors on the Pixel 7a screen were a bit more accurate.

Google Pixel 7a vs. Pixel 6a: Cameras

One of the biggest changes between the Pixel 7a and Pixel 6a is how the back camera is set up. With a 12.2MP main lens and a 12MP ultrawide lens, the Pixel 6a was able to take some pretty good photos, but the Pixel 7a has more sensors.

In particular, the Pixel 7a has a main camera with 64MP and a bigger sensor than the Pixel 6a. Because of this, the Pixel 7a can let in more light, which should make its shots clearer and more detailed. A 13MP sensor is added to the ultrawide camera.

On the front of the Pixel 7a, the selfie camera has been upgraded to 13MP from 8MP on the Pixel 7.

CAMERA

The camera on the Google Pixel 7a is better than on its model. It has a main camera sensor with 64 megapixels and an ultra-wide sensor with 13 megapixels.

The Pixel 6a has a 12.2-megapixel main camera and a 12-megapixel ultra-wide camera, just like the Google Pixel 5. It means that both the main camera and the ultra-wide lens on the Pixel 7a have been updated by Google.

Overall, the Pixel 6a has a great camera. When we tested the Pixel 7a, we found a small software bug, but the results from the camera are great. There are also some great features, like Magic Eraser, which lets you get rid of unwanted items in the background, Real Tone, which makes sure that all skin tones are shown correctly, and Face Unblur, which means that blurry selfies are a thing of the past. They are all on the 7a and 6a.

The front camera sensor on the Pixel 6a is 8 megapixels, but the front camera sensor on the Pixel 7a is 13 megapixels, so there have also been good improvements here.

Ultra-Wide Camera

Pixel 7a   Pixel 6a

The Pixel 7a also has a new ultra-wide camera. In contrast to the Pixel 6a, which uses a 12MP Sony IMX386 sensor, the Pixel 7a uses a 13MP Sony IMX712 sensor for its ultra-wide shots. This could also improve the Pixel 7a's image quality in this camera feature.

Most important, though, is that the Pixel 7a has a much larger field of view, which lets you fit a lot more into your photos. To fit that much on the Pixel 6a, you'd have to take a step back, which isn't always possible. Say you're hiking through a hilly backcountry.

HARDWARE

Like the Pixel 7 and Pixel 7 Pro, the Google Pixel 7a uses the Tensor G2 chip, which is the second version of the Tensor chip. The Pixel 6a, which uses the first-generation Tensor chip, has been improved with this. The Pixel 7a also has a bigger amount of RAM.

The Pixel 6a has a base model with 6GB of RAM and 128GB of storage. The Pixel 7a has a base model with 8GB of RAM and 128GB of storage.

When it comes to the battery, the Pixel 7a also has some changes, but not in terms of how much it can hold. It gets a little less energy life. The Pixel 7a has a 4385mAh battery, which is less than the Pixel 6a, which has a 4500mAh battery. But it can be charged wirelessly with 7.5W, which is a first for a Pixel "a" gadget. The most it can charge with a cable is 18W, which isn't as fast as the Realme GT 3 and it's 240W charging, but most people won't care about that.

STORAGE AND PERFORMANCE

The Pixel 7a is powered by the same Tensor G2 chip that is in the Pixel 7 line. Google's second-generation Tensor is much more efficient than the first model, which means it won't burn like the G1 model did. It also has a more powerful CPU and GPU, which makes it run better.

More importantly, the Tensor G2 uses a newer chip called Exynos 5300, which should make it much easier to connect than the 6a. The latter was known for dropping its mobile network connection at random and for having slow 4G/5G speeds. The Pixel 7a is also faster than its predecessor because it uses the mmWave 5G standard.

Google has increased the Pixel 7a's RAM from 6GB to 8 GB. The extra RAM will help you do more things at once and let you run more apps on the mid-range Pixel 2023 without slowing it down. Google will only sell the phone with 128GB of storage for another year, which is a shame.

Like the 6a, the Pixel 7a will get security patches for five years after it comes out. Google doesn't say much about the OS updates, but like the Pixel 7 and 7 Pro, the Pixel 7a should get three big Android builds.

BATTERY

- Google Pixel 7a has a 4385mAh battery, 18W fast wired charging, and 7.5W wireless charging.
- Google Pixel 6a has a 4410mAh battery and 18W fast wired charge.

The 6a and the 7a almost have the same amount of power in their batteries. There is also no difference in how fast they can charge, as both can charge up to 18W. But because the Pixel 7a has a more powerful Tensor G2 chip, it should last longer than its predecessor.

And because the new Pixel can be charged wirelessly, you can charge it more easily by putting it on a Qi wireless charger. But at 7.5W, the phone will take a long time to fully charge.

QUALITY OF AUDIO AND HAPTICS

In terms of audio and feel, the Pixel 7a is a little bit better than its predecessor. The soundstage is a little bit bigger, and the mids are a little bit louder. The bass isn't very deep or rich, but the sound as a whole is enjoyable.

If you compare it to the Pixel 6a, you might not see such a big change.

Both phones have good vibrations that are neither too sharp nor too muddy.

GOOGLE PIXEL 7A VS PIXEL 6A: SOFTWARE

Both the Pixel 7a and the Pixel 6a run Android 13 with the Pixel skin on top, but the Pixel 7a will give you one more software update. When it came out, the Pixel 6a came with Android 12. This means that it can only be updated to Android 15 and will only get security patches until 2027. The Pixel 7a comes with Android 13 and will be upgraded to Android 16 in the future. Google also says there will be security updates for it for the next five years, so you should be good until 2028.

The Pixel 7a also has some software features that haven't been added to the Pixel 6a yet. Most importantly, it has both a fingerprint scanner and a face unlock feature. This makes it easier to open. Still, the fingerprint reader on the Pixel 7a is much better than the one on the Pixel 6a, so you might not even need to use face unlock if you don't want to.

Also, the Pixel 7a has some of the same features that Google first put in the Pixel 7 and Pixel 7 Pro to make life easier. In the image editing section, you can use Photo Unblur to save pictures that would be too blurry to use otherwise. When you charge your phone overnight next to your bed, you can also use the Pixel 7a's cough and snore recognition, which could help you find health problems you didn't know about.

Aside from that, both the Pixel 7a and Pixel 6a have Google's usual set of great features, such as the At a Glance widget on the home and lock screens that tells you about upcoming calendar events and more, automatic song recognition in the background, transcriptions and speaker labels in Google Recorder, and so much more. Both phones are great because Google is the only company that adds software to them, so they don't have a lot of useless or similar apps. This isn't true of other Android phones.

CHAPTER FOUR

HOW TO SET UP YOUR GOOGLE PIXEL 7A

1. Make sure a 5G SIM is in the device before turning it on.
2. If the device is turned off, press and hold the Power button until you see the Google sign, then let go.

3. Choose the appropriate language from the "Welcome to your Pixel" screen, then touch "Get started."
4. Tap Continue from the 'Phone activation' screen.
- Follow the on-screen instructions after entering the account PIN if necessary
- Make sure the old phone is turned off before activating the new one.
5. Choose a network from the 'Connect to Wi-Fi' menu, then input the password.
- Following setup, tap Skip to add a Wi-Fi network.
6. Choose one of the following options from the 'Copy applications & data' screen:
- Next
- Don't Copy
7. Enter a GoogleTM email address on the "Sign in" screen, then tap "Next."
- After the setup is done, tap Skip to add your Google account.
8. On the 'Who will be using this device' screen, choose the choice you want, then tap Next.

Select when the dot shows up.

- I will use this device.
- My child willing be using this device
9. Tap I Agree on the 'Welcome' screen.
10. On the 'Google Services' screen, choose the options you want and then tap Accept.
11. Choose the choice you want from the "Verizon Services" screen and then tap "I accept."
12. To move on, tap I accept on the screen that says "Additional legal terms."
13. On the 'Set a PIN' screen, enter a PIN code and then tap Next.
- Tap Screen lock settings to set up a pattern or password.
- Tap Skip if you don't want to set up a screen lock, palm recognition, or face recognition.
14. Tap Continue on the "Continue setup" screen to finish setting up your device and make it your own.
- Tap "Leave" and you'll get a reminder to finish it later.
15. Read the information on the "Talk to Google hands-free" screen and tap "I agree" to set up "Hey Google."

- After the activation is done, tap Skip to set up Google Assistant.
16. Tap I agree on the 'Activate Voice Match for Hey Google' screen.
- Tap Skip to go on to the next step.
17. Tap I accept from the 'Access your Assistant without unlocking your device' prompt.
- Simply tap Skip to skip this step.
18. Set up extra things from the "Anything else" screen or tap "No thanks."
19. Tap Yes, I'm in on the screen that says "Get tips and tricks in your email."
20. Tap Try it on the 'Swipe to navigate' screen.
- Tap Skip if you don't want to learn how to use gestures to switch between apps, go Home, and go back.
21. To access the Home screen from the 'All set!' screen, slide up from the phone's bottom.

HOW TO SET UP THE GOOGLE PIXEL 7A FACE UNLOCK

Here's how to enable Face Unlock on your Google Pixel 7a:

1. Unlock the Pixel 7a

Ensure that you are on the phone's home screen and that your Pixel 7a is unlocked.

2. Open the Settings menu

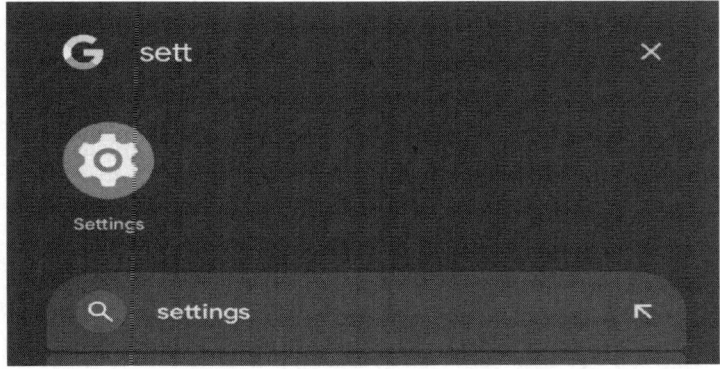

Next, you'll need to get to the phone's Settings app. You can do this by looking for the settings cog icon on your home screen or in your app drawer, or you can look for the same icon in the notification panel.

3. Navigate to Privacy and Security by scrolling down.

Once you're in Settings, scroll down until you see "Security and Privacy," and then tap it.

4. Tap on Lock Device.

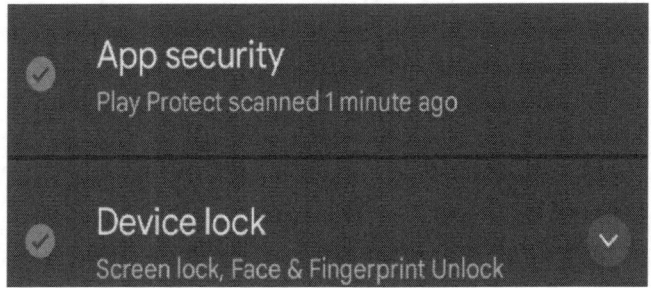

5. Choose Face and Fingerprint.

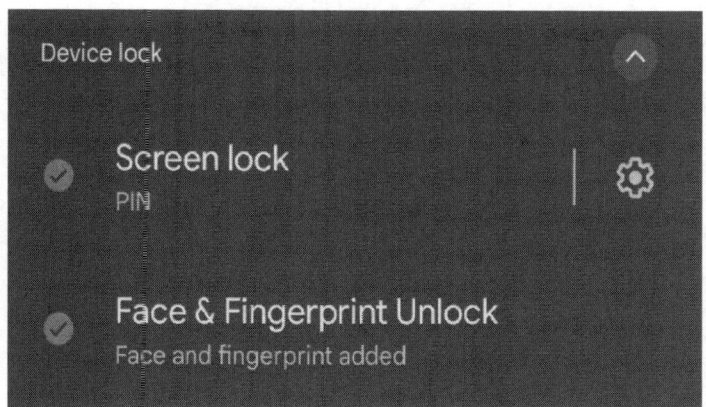

If you have a PIN, enter it now before selecting the Face and Fingerprint Unlock option.

6. Click Face Unlock.

Then, select Face Unlock from the menu. You can also put a fingerprint here if you like.

7. Scan in your face

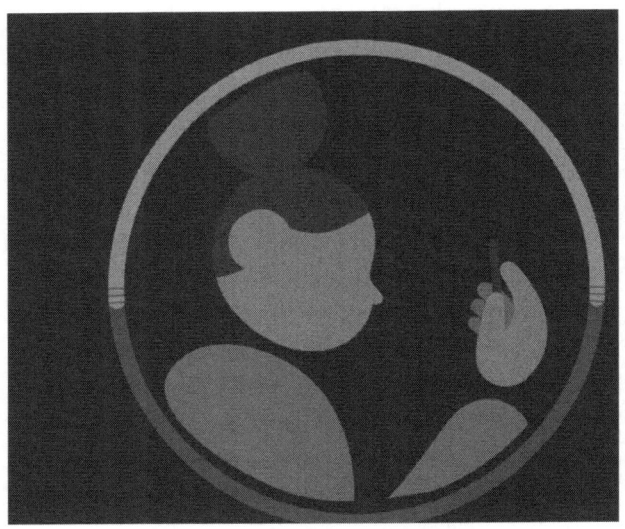

You'll now be taken to a new screen where you must move your face inside a box. If you follow the steps, the front camera will map your face not more than a few seconds should be required. Your face scan has been saved.

SUMMARY

1. Turn the phone on.
2. Open Settings
3. Scroll down to Privacy and Security.
4. Click Device Lock.
5. Choose Face and Fingerprint
6. Tap the Face Unlock
7. Activate Face Unlock

HOW TO TURN ON THE PIXEL 7A 90HZ SCREEN

A 90Hz display is one of the biggest improvements the Pixel 7a has over its predecessor.

Despite having a screen with a 90Hz refresh rate to make scrolling and swiping feel faster, the Pixel 7a by default disables this feature. So, when you first turn on the phone, it will run at 60Hz, just like the Pixel 6a.

Of course, if you want to get the most out of the phone's battery, you should keep it at 60Hz. However, the extra speed is very obvious, and to get the most out of the phone, you should turn it on.

This new feature on the A-series is easy to turn on, and here's how to do it in just a few steps.

1. Get your Pixel 7a unlocked.

First, turn on your Pixel 7a and open it so you can see the home screen.

2. Open Settings

Next, you'll need to open the app called "Settings." This can be done by clicking on the cog icon on the home screen or by pulling down the notification bar and tapping the small cog icon at the bottom.

3. Scroll down to the Display section.

Once you're in Settings, scroll down until you see a choice called "Display." Tap it.

4. Activate Smooth Display

You can change a lot of things in the Display settings, but the one we want to change is Smooth Display. This is what Google calls a setting for a screen that changes between 60Hz and 90Hz. When you tap the Smooth Display area, it will turn on by itself.

Note

Smooth Display does drain the power, but if you turn on the power Saver, the mode will turn off.

CHAPTER FIVE

BASIC SETTINGS TO CHANGE AS SOON AS YOU UNBOX YOUR NEW PIXEL 7A

HOW TO SEND A TEXT TO A FRIEND QUICKLY BY USING VOICE TYPING

Who needs fingers when you can just use your words to type? The original Google Tensor chip, which was used in the Pixel 7a series, made mouth typing on Pixel phones very good. The Pixel 7a line is what the second-generation Tensor G2 builds on and makes better. When you open your keyboard, you'll see a small microphone icon in the top right corner. If you tap this icon, you can type with your mouth.

The Pixel 7a series is very good at listening to what you say and typing it correctly. It even lets you say the names of emojis and quotation marks, which are then added for you. Say "Send" to send a message you've written when you're done. Say "Delete" to get rid of the last word, "Clear" to get rid of the last line, or "Clear all" to get rid of the whole message.

You can use this function to send a text, look for something on Google, or make a note. It's also helpful when you have gloves on or are working without your hands.

UTILIZE THE QUICK TAP GESTURE TO CAPTURE SCREENSHOTS

It's simple to take screenshots with the Quick Tap gestures; all you have to do is flip the phone over and double-tap the back of the device.

Step 1: Select the Quick Tap to start actions under Settings -> System -> Gestures.

Step 2: Next, select the Take Screenshot option to configure the screenshot gesture.

USE DIGITAL WELL-BEING TO GET BETTER AT USING YOUR PHONE.

We all have a confusing relationship with our phones, whether it's doom-scrolling when we're with other people or watching videos late into the night. With the Digital Wellbeing features, Google wants to help you stop being so dependent on your phone and improve how you use it. To access Digital Wellbeing, use the Settings app and navigate down to the section labeled "Digital Wellbeing & parental limits."

Once you're in the Digital Wellbeing area, you'll see a chart that shows how many times you unlocked your phone and how many times you used apps throughout the day. If you use an app too much, you can use an app timer to limit how long you can use it each day. To set a timer for an app, tap the Dashboard option and then tap the hourglass icon to the right of the app's name. Then, choose how long you want to use the app and tap the Okay button.

Bedtime mode can also be set up as part of the Digital Wellbeing suite. Bedtime mode is a feature that makes your phone less useful during the hours you usually sleep or when you want to disconnect. To set this feature up, tap the Bedtime mode option and choose a time for it to start. When Bedtime mode is on, you can set it to instantly turn on Do Not Disturb, limit how often the screen turns on, use grayscale to make your phone easier on the eyes, and set Bedtime mode to turn off when your next alarm goes off.

Google's new cough and snore detection tool is also in bedtime mode. When you turn this function on, your phone can tell how much you snore and cough while Bedtime mode is on. Go to the Bedtime mode area and expand the Weekly average summary to see these numbers.

USE A SHORTCUT TO LAUNCH THE CAMERA RIGHT AWAY.

You can open the camera on the Google Pixel 7a quickly thanks to several handy shortcuts and features. Since this shortcut is already enabled by default, all you have to do to use it is double-press the power button whenever you want on any screen. If the shortcut isn't working, go straight to the settings to enable it. Here is how to activate it.

1. On your Pixel 7a smartphone, go to Settings.
2. Locate the System by sliding it down. As indicated, tap System.
3. At this point, touch on Gestures.
4. After that, tap the choice. Open the camera quickly, then activate the slider.

Now, the Google Pixel 7a cameras may be opened quickly using the shortcut. You may utilize the camera right away by just pressing the power button twice.

CHECK THE PERCENTAGE OF BATTERY LIFE IN THE STATUS BAR.

It's a common complaint that the battery percentage isn't displayed in the upper right corner of the status bar, but if you're familiar with Android, fixing this should be a breeze. The battery % can be displayed in the status bar of your Pixel device with a few simple taps.

First, navigate to the Settings menu on your Pixel.

Second, select Battery from the menu.

Third, use the slider labeled "Battery percentage" to adjust the battery level.

If you slide this to the On position, the smartphone's status bar will include the battery percentage. Following the same procedures as above, you can disable the percentage by toggling it to the Off position. If you own a Pixel 7a device, this is the simplest way to check the remaining battery life.

HOW TO MAKE PIXEL 7A'S TOUCH SENSITIVE

1. Go to the Settings menu on your Pixel 7a phone.

2. Tap the choice that says Display settings when you find it.
3. Scroll down until you find the choice for "Screen Protector Mode."
4. Turn the switch for the choice on to make it work.

HOW TO CHANGE SCREEN RESOLUTION

The 6.7-inch 2K+ LTPO AMOLED curved screen of the Pixel 7a is among the brightest and boasts one of the highest contrast ratios of any smartphone display. Even though the Pixel 7a has fantastic battery life, you may choose between two different display resolutions: the higher QuadHD+ resolution or the lower FullHD+ resolution. Here's how to adjust the Google Pixel 7 Pro's display settings.

Most phones have a default resolution, but what if you want to lock in either a high-quality QuadHD+ display or a more power-efficient FullHD+ display? As you can see in your Pixel's display settings, adjusting the resolution is as simple as tapping a button. Check out these simple instructions for how to proceed.

First, navigate to the Settings menu on your Pixel.

Second, select "Display" from the available options.

Third, above the Smooth Display option, select Screen Resolution.

Fourth, select either "High resolution" or "Full resolution" from the "Screen resolution" menu. FullHD+ (1080p) is considered High, whereas QHD+ or 2K+ (1440p) is considered Full.

Battery life can be preserved or increased by selecting the High resolution, but a sharp, high-quality display can be achieved by selecting the Full resolution. The higher the screen resolution, the more battery power is needed on the phone, so you'll need to make that decision carefully.

GESTURE-ACTIVATED FLASHLIGHT ON/OFF

How do you activate the phone's flashlight? A quick shortcut in the notification shade is used by the vast majority of Android users we know. However, how quickly do you think you can activate the phone's flashlight? Quickly activate the flashlight with a double touch on the back using the Quick touch gesture. With the new Pixel 7a, accomplishing such a feat is child's play.

1. To enable gesture controls, navigate to the system's preferences then choose "Gestures."
2. Assign the Quick Tap gesture to the Toggle flashlight by tapping on it.

To activate the flashlight, double-tap the back of the phone. It's a piece of cake, right?

HOW TO ACTIVATE NOW PLAYING
1. Navigate to the Settings menu.
2. Launch the search window and enter "now playing."
3. Toggle the setting to On by tapping the first result.

SET UP RULES TO AUTOMATE YOUR DEVICE

You can automate certain tasks on your Pixel 7a by adding prompts that are based on where you are. For example, you can use Rules to set your phone to "Do Not Disturb" when you get to the office or to "Silent" when you get home.

Under Settings > System > Rules, you can change your device's state based on its location or Wi-Fi. So, when your Pixel connects to your home's Wi-Fi network, it can automatically switch to vibrate or ringer mode, based on what you want.

MacroDroid is a good place to start if you want to set up advanced programming on your Android device. You can also use IFTTT applets to control your Android phone.

USE LIVE TRANSLATION ON THE PHONE, IN VIDEOS, AND OTHER

The Live Translate feature on the Pixel 7 is helpful because it can translate text chats and videos in real-time into several different languages. The best thing is that the feature works even when you are not online. Live Translate will make it easy to talk to friends and family who don't speak the same language as you do.

Text, the camera, videos, podcasts, phone calls, video calls, and even voice messages may all be translated with Live Translate. In apps that allow it, you will automatically see a Translate button. When you click it, the text or audio will be translated into English or the language you speak.

In apps that allow it, a pop-up will show up and translate the text on the screen into the language you choose. Keep in mind that for some languages, you will only be able to get live translation through the camera, and they might not support Interpreter Mode or Live Caption.

HOW TO TURN ON "ONE-HAND MODE"

With a 6.7-inch screen, the Pixel 7 is a pretty big phone. Because the display has a big footprint, you can't reach the corner with your thumb without doing some finger gymnastics or using your other hand as a support.

In these scenarios, you might want to use the device's one-handed mode, which is also available on the regular Pixel 7a. It will move the information on the screen to the bottom of the screen, where it will be easier to reach with one hand.

You must first turn on one-handed mode by going to Settings > System > Gestures > One-handed mode. To turn on the mode, you have to swipe down near the bottom part of the screen. Note that this shortcut will only work on your Pixel if you use gesture control.

HOW TO CHANGE YOUR QUICK SETTINGS SO THAT SHORTCUTS ARE EASY TO ACCESS

Swiping down from the top of the screen brings up the fast settings menu. Use the pencil icon to add the settings you use the most to this menu. Google gives you a lot of choices, like saving battery life, turning on and off the microphone, and getting to your alarms. Here you will find basic goods like airplane mode, Bluetooth, and Wi-Fi.

CONFIGURE SAFETY FEATURES LIKE HEADS-UP AND CRASH DETECTION

Your Pixel 7a is equipped to recognize when you've been in an accident. Of course, this is nothing new because Pixels have had this function for a while. You must access the Safety app to turn it on. You will be required to provide emergency contact information in addition to other details such as blood type and medical issues. Then, select Turn On next to Crash Detection by scrolling down.

The other useful safety feature is not just that. For people who have the unfortunate habit of walking while glancing at their phone, Heads Up was created. If it notices you're moving around while looking at your phone directly, it regularly sends you alerts. To activate it:

1. Go to Settings, then Digital Wellbeing and Parental Controls, and then click on "Heads Up."
2. When it asks for permission, tap next and say yes to be able to view your location and physical activity.
3. You will tap next again, then tap done.

TURN ON THE ADAPTIVE ALERT VIBRATION MODE

Most of the Pixel 7a's features are also available on other Pixel phones, but this one is really special. With adaptive alert vibration, you can lower the strength of the vibration when your phone is still and the screen is facing up. The idea is that you'll see the screen even if the shaking isn't as strong.

It's very easy to turn on:

1. Open the app for Settings.

2. Scroll down until you see Sound & Vibration > Vibrations & Haptics. Tap on it.
3. Turn on the sound for the adaptive alert.

All done. You can't control exactly how much the sounds from notifications are turned down because Google does that for you. Remember that this tool works for both alerts and alarms.

CHANGE BETWEEN THE FRONT AND BACK CAMERAS WITH A SIMPLE TWIST

Did you know that you can quickly switch between the front and back cameras on your phone by turning it like a screwdriver? It's simple once you figure it out. Go to Settings > System > Gestures > Flip camera for a selfie to turn on the feature.

MAKE THE MOST OF GOOGLE'S PHOTOGRAPHY AND CAMERA TOOLS.

The Pixel 7a's camera and photography software are its main selling points. The Pixel 7a camera is capable of a wide range of tasks. For improved nighttime photography, there are tools like Night Sight and Magic Eraser, as well as many others.

Photo Unblur is a feature we simply must promote. Photo Unblur not only uses AI to eliminate fuzzy parts from your photos but it can also be used on previously taken pictures. Our user manual provides clearer instructions on how to operate Photo and Face Unblur.

But you can do much more than that! The capability to shoot in RAW or even the addition of grid lines to your viewfinder are some other amazing camera capabilities.

You only need to carry out the following easy steps to shoot in RAW:

1. Tap the Settings icon in the upper-left corner of the Camera app after opening it.
2. Select Advanced from the More Settings menu by tapping it.
3. Turn on the RAW+JPEG control.

HOW TO SET UP GRID LINES

1. Return to the Camera app's settings page.
2. Select More Settings.
3. Go to Composition and select Grid type.
4. Choose between the golden ratio, 33, and 44.

HOW TO GET RID OF AN ALARM OR PHONE CALL WITHOUT SAYING "HEY GOOGLE"

All of us were there. It's 6:00, and your alarm starts to go off. You're so tired that you can barely get to the phone. With the Pixel 6, Google makes this a little easier by letting you stop or turn off an alarm by saying "Snooze" or "Stop" instead of "Hey Google." You can do the same thing with your phone by saying "Answer" or "Reject" instead of picking it up.

Open the Settings menu and click on Apps to turn it on. Then choose Assistant and tap Quick Prayers. You should be able to get new calls, and set alarms, and timers. To turn each one on, touch the switch next to it.

ADD A GOOGLE ACCOUNT THAT ALREADY EXISTS

1. To view all apps, scroll up from the Home screen.
2. Go to the Settings Settings icon and click on Passwords and accounts.
3. Click Add account, and then click Google.

If asked, enter the current way of locking (Fingerprint, PIN, etc.) to continue.

4. After entering your Gmail address, select "Next."
5. Tap Next after you've put in the right password.
6. If "Keep your account updated with this phone's number" shows up, read it and tap "Yes, I'm in" or "Skip" to move on.
7. Review the Terms of Service and Privacy Policy, and then tap "I agree" to move forward.
8. If given the chance, you can turn on or off any of the following:
- If there is a tick, it is turned on.
- Save the apps on your phone.
- App info Settings Personal dictionaries
- Wi-Fi passwords.

9. You can go back by swiping left along the bottom edge, or you can leave by swiping up from the bottom.

TRANSFER PHOTOS OR VIDEOS TO YOUR COMPUTER

1. To connect your phone to a computer, use the USB cord that was included with it.
2. Open either 'File Explorer' or 'Windows Explorer'.
3. Using File Explorer or Windows Explorer, go to Pixel 7a Internal shared storage.
4. Use the computer to copy video or picture files from the following folders to the intended folder(s) on the computer's hard drive:
- DCIM\
- Camera
- Download
- Movies
- Pictures
5. Remove the USB cables from your computer.

METHODS FOR TRANSFERRING DATA FROM PIXEL TO PIXEL

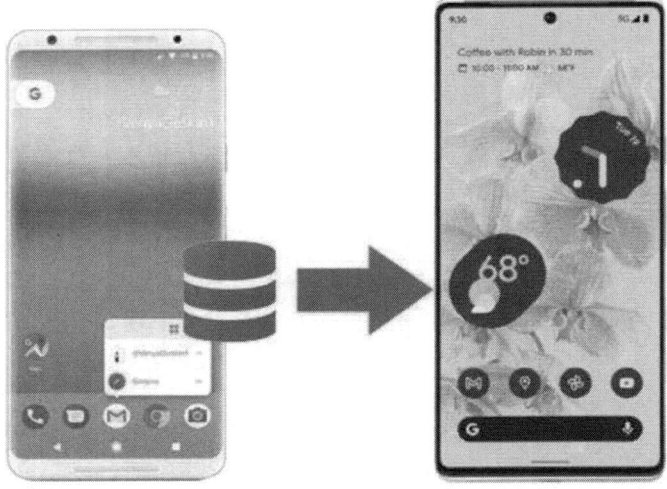

Google's Quick Switch Adapter is a method for copying data from Pixel to Pixel. It's important to note that your Google Pixel phone already comes with the Pixel data transfer tool pre-loaded and doesn't need to be manually installed. However, there are some files that you cannot transmit during setup.

What you can transfer:

- Apps and their data
- Accounts on Google
- Phone contacts or SIM card contacts

- Photographs, music, and video
- The history of phone calls
- SMS and multimedia text messages
- Phone configurations
- Wallpapers

What you are unable to transfer:

- Photos, music, and movies are stored in secret folders.
- Apps not found in the Google Play Store
- Instead of Google accounts and their data, app data does not employ Android backup accounts.
- Downloaded files, such as PDF Ringtones
- Contacts and calendars synchronized with services other than Google
- Certain phone configurations

Before you begin, make certain of the following:

- Your Pixel phones have been completely charged.
- Your Pixel phone comes with an adapter and a USB cable.
- A dependable Wi-Fi network

- SIM card security code
- A working Google account

To move from Pixel to Pixel:

1. Make sure the old Pixel phone has been upgraded to the most recent version.

2. Turn on your new Pixel phone and select Get Started. Then, take your old phone's SIM card and insert it into the new phone.

3. Register your new Pixel phone with a reliable Wi-Fi or mobile network. Later, on the Copy applications & data screen, tap Next, and then switch on your old Pixel phone.

4. Connect both phones using the USB cable and adaptor. Next, on your new Pixel phone, enter your Google account password and tap Sign in.

5. Uncheck the files you do not wish to transfer and then click the Copy button.

6. When the transfer process is finished, click Done.

CHAPTER SIX

CAMERA

The Pixel 7a's dual camera system consists of a 64MP primary camera with an f/1.89 aperture and a 1/1.73" sensor and a 13MP ultrawide camera with an f/2.2 aperture.

FEATURES OF GOOGLE PIXEL 7A CAMERAS

The Pixel 7a has three camera modules that are better than before. The main camera is now a 64MP sensor with pixel binning, the 13MP ultrawide has a bigger 120-degree field of view and autofocus, and the 13MP selfie camera has a wider 95-degree angle so you can fit more people or more background in the shot.

Notably, the main 64MP sensor has smaller pixels than the Pixel 6a and Pixel 7 (0.8 microns vs. 1.4 microns and 1.2 microns, respectively), so each pixel catches less light. The binning process, which combines four pixels next to each other into one to make a 16MP picture, makes up for some of this.

Even though the pixels on the 7a are smaller, Google still put 8x Super Res Zoom on it, just like on the Pixel 7. Even at 8x zoom, you can get 16MP shots by cropping the 64MP sensor and using digital zoom.

Also, the Pixel 7a has some features from the more expensive Pixel 7 series. These include a faster night mode, a new long exposure mode for fun effects like wavy water or traffic light streaks, Magic Eraser, and the great Photo Unblur, which can clean up and sharpen any photo, old or new. But there are no action pans, so you can't "freeze" a car or bike in the middle of the road like you can with the Pixel 7 series.

Like all modern Pixels, it has a mode for astrophotography with time-lapses, a panorama, and Photo Sphere mode, and a 1x and 2x portrait mode. Google's Top Shot, Frequent Faces, and Face Unblur will help you get the best picture possible, no matter how much your subjects move while you take the picture. And the camera app has its signature framing tips to help you line up your shots better, two exposure sliders for brightness and shadows, and a custom white balance slider.

The video also got some improvements compared to the Pixel 6a in every way. The ultrawide lens can now capture 4K footage at 30 frames per second and perform 1080p dramatic pans. The selfie camera can now record 4K video at 30fps and 1080p at 60fps. There is no 10-bit HDR, audio zoom, or cinematic blur mode. Those are still only on the Pixel 7 and 7 Pro. However, there are still slow-motion and timelapse modes, as well as normal, locked, active, and cinematic pan stabilization modes.

GOOGLE PIXEL 7A CAMERAS SHOOTOUT

The Pixel 7a works equally well as the Pixel 6a and Pixel 7 in bright, outdoor settings. With the identical color science, exposure balance, and clarity across the three phones, the two photographs are essentially indistinguishable from one another. However, if you look closely, you'll see that the Pixel 7a's 80-degree field of view is exactly halfway between the Pixel 7's 82-degree and Pixel 6A's 77-degree ranges.

VERY SOLID HDR PERFORMANCE

The Pixel 7a begins to demonstrate some of its strengths in exposures that are more difficult. When compared to the Pixel 7a and Pixel 7 shots, the Pixel 6a shot is noticeably noisier. The overall photo leans somewhat yellower/greener thanks to the 6a's overexposure of the clouds as well. Pixel binning enables the 7a and 7 to capture more detail and achieve a stronger contrast between the brighter sky and the darker areas of the cat sculpture.

EXCELLENT NIGHTTIME AND LOW-LIGHT PHOTOGRAPHY

In conditions of low light, the Pixel 7a surpasses the Pixel 6a. You can notice that it captures better clarity with less noise in this purple hour image even without the night mode being turned on. It comes close to the higher Pixel 7 in quality.

Pixel 7a   Pixel 6a   Pixel 7

This difference is more noticeable at night when the quicker Night Sight option of the Pixel 7a shines. During my testing of the three Pixels, the 7a focused and captured pictures just as quickly as the 7, whereas the 6a took a good one to two seconds to even initiate the capture before taking twice as long to do so. The Pixel 6a pushes the highlights too far and exhibits minimal contrast compared to the other two, whereas the Pixel 7a's photos are more evenly distributed and clearer than both. I would rank the Pixel 7a higher here than the 7 if it weren't for the more obvious lens flare.

Pixel 7a Night Sight	Pixel 6a	Pixel 7

ENHANCED NIGHT SIGHT

According to Google, Night Sight, the night mode on Pixel Phones, is now twice as quick as the Pixel 6a. This implies that the time it takes to take pictures in Night Sight mode will be shortened.

LONG EXPOSURE

The Pixel 7a now supports the Long Exposure function, allowing users to select to take pictures that give the impression of motion, for the first time in Google's midrange "a" series of smartphones.

HIGH RES ZOOM

Super Res Zoom was always believed to be a function available only on Google's more costly phone models, but the company has now managed to introduce this feature to the Pixel 7a as well. Super Res Zoom now allows users to zoom in up to 8 times.

NEW CAMERA FOR SELFIES

All of the cameras on the Pixel 7a are being updated, including the one on the front. The Pixel 7a's new selfie camera has 13 MP, a field of view of 95 degrees, and the ability to take video at 4K 30 FPS. It also has support for Face Unlock, which is great!

The Pixel 7a has how many cameras?

The Pixel 7a has the same number of cameras as its models, which are three: a main camera, an ultra-wide camera, and a front-facing camera for taking selfies.

GOOGLE PIXEL 7A CAMERA VS GOOGLE PIXEL 7 CAMERA

PIXEL 7 VS PIXEL 7A: CAMERA SPECS

First, let's look at the Pixel 7, which came out in October 2022. The main camera has 50 megapixels, and there is also a wide-angle camera with 12 megapixels. There is also a laser autofocus sensor and a spectral anti-flicker sensor. The main camera has a Super Res Zoom of 8x, and the wide-angle camera has a field of view (FOV) of 114 degrees. The Pixel 7 has both optical image stabilization (OIS) and electronic image stabilization (EIS), as well as a 10.8MP fixed-focus face camera.

The Pixel 7a is a little different. Instead of a 50MP camera, it has a 64MP main camera, which still lets you zoom in 8 times. This isn't an optical zoom, but it uses Google's software skills to make sure that zoomed-in photos look as good as possible. The 120-degree FOV wide-angle camera has 13MP, OIS, EIS, and phase detection autofocus. The 13MP front-facing camera has a fixed focus.

When you look deeper into the requirements, you find other differences. The Pixel 7 has 1.2nm pixels, while the Pixel 7a has 0.8nm pixels. The Pixel 7a's aperture is f/1.89, while the Pixel 7's aperture is f/1.85. The Pixel 7a's sensor is 1/1.73 inches, while the Pixel 7's sensor is 1/1.31 inches. The Pixel 7a also automatically saves shots with more pixels than the Pixel 7. The resolution of a Pixel 7a photo is 4624 by 3472 pixels, whereas that of a Pixel 7 photo is 4080 by 3072.

PIXEL 7 VS PIXEL 7A: MAIN CAMERA
Even though the main cameras on the two phones are different, there isn't much difference between the pictures. You'll only notice a difference if you compare the photos side by side and pick them apart. Either phone

is fine if you rarely use the secondary camera; the primary camera is plenty for most people. This needs to be said right off the bat, as does the fact that I've gone out of my way to locate new and intriguing topics to photograph with my Pixel 7 and Pixel 7a and how much I've enjoyed doing so. Some of the pictures were taken in the U.K. during the weekend of King Charles's coronation. I was glad to have Pixel phones because I knew the pictures I took would be of great quality. I love how they both make me feel creative and full of confidence.

1. Google Pixel 7
2. Google Pixel 7a

In the first picture, the Pixel 7a shows some deeper colors, but this is not a pattern because the Pixel 7 can sometimes do the same thing.

Even the tread pattern on the tires of the Triumph Stag is the same. This is an amazing level of detail. The Pixel 7 has a better white balance and contrast than the Pixel 7a, but the change is so small that it's hard to say which one is better.

1. Google Pixel 7
2. Google Pixel 7a

This is also clear in the second photo. The Pixel 7 picture brings out the white side panels of the van more than the Pixel 7a photo does, and the colors may be a little bit brighter. But the amount of detail, the tone, and the atmosphere are all the same. You have to look closely and zoom in to see the noise in the Pixel 7a's clouds, but most people won't care too much about it.

1. Google Pixel 7
2. Google Pixel 7a

The picture of the muffin shows the depth of field that can be achieved with the main camera when the conditions are right. It also shows how detailed both cameras can be. Again, the Pixel 7's picture has a better white balance, but the Pixel 7a's photo has a better overall tone, and a small edit to boost the exposure would make it stand out. In general, the Pixel 7a takes better close-up shots than the Pixel 7, which didn't always focus well.

1. Google Pixel 7
2. Google Pixel 7a

The final picture has fewer differences in color, contrast, and white balance, and if the Pixel 7a's photo has any extra noise, you have to look very closely to see it. Both photos show the scene pretty much the same way, and the changes don't make one better than the other.

CHAPTER SEVEN

MESSAGES

HOW TO USE GOOGLE PIXEL PHONES' AUDIO MESSAGE TRANSCRIPTION FEATURE

Audio messages can be useful, but sometimes they can be very annoying. You can't listen to them in a school or office full of people, for example. Google has added a tool that translates voice messages, no matter what your reason is.

On compatible devices, Audio Message Transcription is turned on by default. If it's not, open the Messages app, tap on your image, and go to Message settings > Voice message transcription to turn it on. Toggle Show the written versions of text mails. The next time you receive a voice message through the Google Messages app, you'll be able to access more options by tapping the plus sign that appears above the voice memo. Just expand it, and the copy should show up.

How to Use Transcription of an Audio Message

On machines that can do it, Audio Message Transcription should be turned on by default. The next time you get a speech message on Google Messages, there will be a box above it that you can expand. Tap on it to make it bigger. You can see the text that was typed there.

1. Receive a sound message on Google Messages.
2. Right above the voice message, you should see a box that you can expand. Touch it.
3. There will be the text that has been typed out.
4. You can also tap the button in this text box that says "Hide."

How to turn on or off Audio Message Transcription

Audio Message Transcription can be turned on or off in a few different ways. You can do it in the settings for Google Messages or by using a copy.

Google Messages settings:

1. Open the app called "Google Messages."

2. Tap on the picture of you.
3. Choose Settings for messages.
4. Go into Voice message transcription.
5. Toggle Turn on or off the recording of voice mails.

From the message's transcription:

1. Get a voice message through Google Messages.
2. Increase the size of the box.
3. Tap the gear button in the box where you type.
4. Toggle Turn on or off the recording of voice mails.

HOW TO SEND A MESSAGE

1. Open the app for Voice.
2. Open the Messages tab, then tap the Compose button.
3. Tap the name of the person you want to text from your list of friends.
4. Enter your message at the bottom, and then tap Send.

HOW TO QUICKLY DELETE SMS ON A PIXEL PHONE

1. Launch the built-in Messages app.

2. Tap the profile symbol in the upper right corner of the screen.

3. Select Settings for Messages.

4. Select Swipe Actions by scrolling down.

5. Select Customize for Right or Left Swipe. Actions include Off, Delete, and Archive.

HOW TO GET DELETED TEXTS BACK ON A GOOGLE PIXEL PHONE

If you have ever synced your text messages to your Google account, you can get back lost messages by following the steps below.

1. Go to Settings > Reset on your Google Pixel phone.

2. Click "Start" to set up your device, and then follow the steps on the screen. When you get to the Copy apps and data screen, click Copy apps and data > Next > Can't use old phone > OK > A backup from the cloud.

3. Sign into the same Google account you used to back up your messages, choose the most current backup file from the list, and click the Restore option.

Wait until the process of repair is done.

HOW TO USE GOOGLE PIXEL'S BUILT-IN BACKUP TO GET BACK DELETED TEXTS

You can only use this way if you have turned on the Google Pixel feature that lets you back up and restore your phone.

1. Go to your Google Pixel phone's settings.

2. Go to Google and click Services. Then click Restore Messages. Then, pick the friends that you want to bring back.

3. Click "Restore" and wait until it tells you "Messages Restored."

Again, is it possible to get back the SMS that has been deleted? Yes. And you can see that backing up and restoring your Google Pixel phone is the best way to get deleted text messages back. So, make sure to back up your device often from now on.

HOW TO RECOVER DELETED SMS ON GOOGLE PIXEL WITHOUT BACKUP USING COOLMUSTER ANDROID SMS + CONTACTS RECOVERY

Coolmuster Android SMS + Contacts Recovery is another way to get back lost texts without a backup. This pure SMS recovery app can, as its name suggests, recover deleted text messages and contacts straight from the Google Pixel's internal memory and SIM card. And you can look at, choose, recover, and back up both texts and contacts that are already there and ones that have been removed from the computer.

In the same way, it works with all Android phones running Android 2.0 or higher.

1. After installing Coolmuster Android SMS + Contacts Recovery on your computer, open the program and go to the tools. From there, select the SMS + Contacts Recovery module.
2. Use a USB connection to connect the Google Pixel to your computer. Once the computer knows what your device is, it will instantly install the driver on the device. When this program asks what type of data you want to recover, select "Messages" and then proceed by following the on-screen instructions.

Notes: If you want to see all of your SMS on Google Pixel, you have to root your phone first.

3. After scanning, choose Messages from the panel on the left, check the messages you want from the panel on the right, and then tap Recover below to get your lost Google text messages back.

CHAPTER EIGHT

PHOTOS

The cameras on our new Pixel 7A are great for capturing your moments, but taking photos is just the start. We all want our shots to look great so we can share them and look back on them. Machine learning has made it possible for Google Photos to have powerful editing tools that are easy to use.

USE PHOTO UNBLUR TO FIX SHOTS THAT ARE BLURRY

Photo Unblur is a brand-new tool that is only available on the Pixel 7A. With just a few taps, you can make a blurry photo clear again. With Photo Unblur, you may restore photos to their original clarity by eliminating blur and visual noise. Best of all, it works with scanned images and pictures you took with a different phone or camera.

How to use Photo Unblur

1. Open the Google Photos app and choose a picture.

Choose an image that you'd want to unblur from your collection if your Google Photos app is current. When the image has expanded, select Edit from the bottom menu by tapping on it.

Notably, Photo Unblur only functions on still images—not moving pictures like videos.

2. Utilizing Photo Unblur

There are two methods to use this to access the Photo Unblur tool. The toggle for this feature will show up in the Suggestions tab if Google determines that the photo is fuzzy, to begin with. Alternatively, select Unblur from the Tools menu. In both situations, after you choose Unblur, the app will buffer for a good 2-3 seconds as it analyzes the different lines, curves, and components of your shot before remastering it to make the subject(s) more distinct.

3. Changing the filter's sensitivity and saving

The final product will display at the 100% filter level, meaning further sharpening is not possible or recommended. The Pixel's maximum output was generally sufficient and startlingly realistic-looking.

But since not all modifications will be perfect, you can still lower the filter level to make the result look less fake or crisp. You can pinch into your photo while in the editing menu to see the changes more clearly.

When you are happy with the correction, hit Done, followed by Save. You'll have a copy of the unblurred image in addition to the original for archival purposes.

USE A MAGIC ERASER TO GET RID OF DISTRACTIONS

Magic Eraser came out last year, and you can find things in your pictures that are distracting, like people in the background, power lines, and power poles. It only took a few taps to get rid of them, and they were gone. You can also use a circle or a brush to get rid of something. Don't worry about being exact. Magic Eraser will figure out what you want to get rid of.

Extra Magic Eraser tip: Don't want to get rid of something completely, but just want it to fit in a bit more? Use the Camouflage tool in

Magic Eraser to change the color of things in your picture that is getting in the way. With just a few taps, the object's colors and outlines look like they belong in the picture.

USE PORTRAIT BLUR TO MAKE YOUR SUBJECT STAND OUT.

With the Pixel Camera's Portrait setting, your subject can stand out. But what if you forgot to use it when you took a picture, or if you want to change an old picture? Portrait blur lets Google Photos hide the background of photos of people, pets, food, flowers, and more, even after they've been taken.

USE PORTRAIT LIGHT TO IMPROVE THE LIGHT ON FACES

Taking a high-quality photo is challenging for several reasons, including poor lighting and the use of an outdated device. Portrait light makes it easy to improve the lighting on faces, and you can even change where and how bright the light is to make your look unique.

SKY IDEAS CAN CHANGE THE MOOD AND TONE OF YOUR SUNSET PHOTOS.

You probably have quite a few photos of sunsets that don't quite do justice to how beautiful they were at the time. How do you bring it back to life and make it stand out? Use sky ideas to give your golden hour photos your creative spin. You can choose from different themes that change the color and contrast of the sky to change the mood and tone of your photo and get it ready to share.

USE THE COLLAGE TOOL TO CREATE THINGS THAT CAN BE SHARED.

With the new collage editor, you can make creative images that you can share. Pixel users can pick up to six photos and choose from more than 50 styles. You can easily change the plan by dragging and dropping, and you can also edit each photo in the collage separately to get the look you want.

Mix and match all of these features to make a beautiful picture that's ready to share. Using Photo Unblur, Portrait light, and Portrait blur, you can eliminate a distracting background subject and recreate a vivid memory.

HOW TO CHANGE THE COLOR OF THE SKY IN GOOGLE PHOTOS

1. Open the Google Photos application.
2. Locate the picture you want to change. It should, of course, depict the sky.

3. Click Edit.
4. the Tools tab, please.
5. Select Sky.
6. Choose the effect that you want to use. Vivid, Luminous, Radiant, Ember, Airy, Afterglow, and Stormy are the available options.
7. To change the intensity of the effect, move the slider.
8. When ready, click Done.
9. Choose to Save a copy.

CHAPTER NINE

TRANSFER OF DATA

Right now, Google Pixel phones are all the rage, and they have a loyal following. Many fans can't wait for the next Pixel to come out so they can update it. But switching phones every year or even more often can make it hard to move all your info.

Even if you don't get a new Pixel phone, it's always useful to know how to move info from one Pixel phone to another. This is especially true if you have friends who also have Pixel phones. Lucky for you, there are many ways to do it, and you can choose the one you like best. In different situations, different methods can also be useful. Let's figure it out.

After setup, is it possible to transfer data to Google Pixel?

Yes, you can transfer all of your data to the Google Pixel once you've set it up. This is easy to do when you set up your new phone, but you can always do it later if you didn't.

If you always back up all the information on the phone you use, all you need to do on your new Pixel phone is log in to your Google account. You can find the "Restore Backup" option in your settings if you want to recover a backup from another phone. When you do this, your contacts, calendar information, passwords, etc. will be delivered to your new phone.

5 METHODS FOR TRANSFERRING DATA FROM ONE PIXEL TO ANOTHER

There are many ways to transfer data from Pixel to Pixel, regardless of whether you are switching to a new phone or simply transferring data. Let's examine a few different approaches so you can understand when to use each one.

USE THE GOOGLE DATA TRANSFER TOOL APP

On Google Pixel phones, there is a data transfer utility app already loaded. When switching from an old Pixel phone to a new Pixel phone, you can utilize the Google Pixel Transfer Tool to transfer all of your data. Keep in mind that this technique only functions if the target phone is a Pixel. How?

1. Connect both Pixel phones.

To connect both of your phones, a cable, and an adaptor are required. You will need the cord and adapter to connect two phones because this software only supports wired connections. Launch the Data Transfer Tool app once you've linked the phones.

2. Transferring Data from an Existing Phone Once the app has been launched, select "Transfer Data from an Existing Phone" and then press the "Next" button. If you choose to transfer your data, a popup should appear on your phone as a result.
3. Grant Permission

Accept the popup and give consent to start the data transmission. You have the option of choosing what data to transfer and what not to. After that, simply tap the Copy button.

USE AIRDROID PERSONAL

With AirDroid, you may transfer data between Google Pixel devices of any kind as well as from other Android or iOS devices. You can transfer whatever type of data you desire without a cable. This is how:1.

1. Download and set up AirDroid.

On both Pixel phones, you must first download and set up your AirDroid account. Ask your friend to reciprocate if you're sharing files with them.

2. Log in to your AirDroid accounts.

The next step is to sign into AirDroid. This is how AirDroid makes wireless data transfers simple.

3. Access the File

Open the document or data that you want to send to the other Pixel phone. After selecting the choices button, select the Send icon.

4. Distribute the file.

You can choose your device name from the list of people you can share with after being redirected to the AirDroid software, and then you're done!

USE BLUETOOTH

An ancient method of sharing data is Bluetooth, which is compatible with Pixel and pretty much every other phone. It has a size restriction and is extremely sluggish and unreliable. But here's how to use it if you want to.

1. Enable Bluetooth.

By swiping down and selecting the Bluetooth symbol from the drag-down menu on your home screen, you can activate your Bluetooth. Keep in mind to confirm that the other device's Bluetooth is activated as well.

2. Connect the Devices

A new device can be connected by opening your Bluetooth settings and selecting it. It should be immediately visible if Bluetooth is enabled and functioning properly on the other Pixel. To connect, tap on it.

3. Distribute the file.

Next, locate and open the file you wish to send. After clicking the choices box, select "Share." The Bluetooth icon ought to appear.

Touch it. Send the file to the second Pixel device after that.

UTILIZE GOOGLE DRIVE

A fairly cool method of transferring files between several devices is Google Drive. When auto-backup is enabled, switching to a new phone is quite simple because all of your data is accessible by simply signing into your Google Account. The alternative is to manually transfer data between Pixel devices using this.

1. Upload the File

From your Pixel phone, you may manually upload any file to Google Drive so that you can access it from any location. Navigate to the file, select settings, and then choose Share. On the Drive symbol, tap.

2. Choose the location

You will be prompted by Google Drive to choose the place where you want to save your file. You have the option of saving it directly or in a new folder. Ensure that you can locate it later.

3. Share the file.

There are now numerous options available for you to obtain this file. You may quickly locate this file by launching the Drive app on your other Pixel phone if you are signed in to your Google Account. Otherwise, you can launch the Drive app on your phone and tap on Options while the file is open. To copy the link to the file, choose Copy Link.

Then, if you use a separate Google account on your new Pixel phone, you may mail the link to yourself or send it to anybody you choose.

Click the link to access the file.

USE A COMPUTER

This is a more conventional method for those of you who like things the old-fashioned way. A computer can act as a middleman when transferring files between Pixel phones. Contacts, settings, and a few other types of data will not be compatible with this. It works best for moving pictures, music, etc.

1. Connect your old phone to the computer Connect your Pixel phone to your PC via a USB cord. Both phones can be connected at once or separately. You should get a pop-up asking what you

wish to do after your PC detects the phone. To view files, click Open Folder.
2. Copy the file

Next, navigate to the file you wish to copy, and drag it there before dropping it on your desktop. If both of your Pixel phones are linked, you can also just directly copy it to that phone's folder. If not, you may simply connect your new phone to the PC and transfer the file by dragging it from the desktop to the phone.

HOTE

Each of the various methods for transferring data across Pixels may be valuable for you, depending on your circumstances. Using the Data Transfer app is an excellent choice, for instance, if you're migrating to a new phone. In all other cases, AirDroid is a fantastic choice because it offers you the freedom that the other approaches lack.

FAQs

1. Can data be transferred from one Pixel to another without an internet connection?

No, you don't require the internet to use the Google Data Transfer Tool app. But a cable connection would be necessary for any approach that doesn't use the internet. With the aid of the internet, using a wireless connection is much simpler.

2. Is it possible to move data from an iPhone to a Pixel?

Yes, you may use the AirDroid app to transfer all of your data from an iPhone to a Pixel. It is incredibly simple to use and functions on both systems. Just manually share it with others.

3. What should you do if your old Pixel phone won't let you transfer data to it?

If you are setting up your Pixel and can't send data, check the cable to see if it works right. Pull it out and put it back in, then try again. If that doesn't work, you can recover your backups using Google Drive.

CHAPTER TEN

BACK UP YOUR GOOGLE PIXEL PHONE AND RESTORE IT

The robust hardware, user-friendly interface, and easy Google service integration make Google Pixel phones popular. However, just like any other smartphone, Pixel phones are also susceptible to data loss from hardware failure, software bugs, or unintentional deletion. To ensure that your key data, like photos, contacts, and messages, are secure and quickly recoverable in case of any unforeseen circumstances, it is essential to routinely back up your Pixel phone.

I'll walk you through the process of backing up and restoring a Google Pixel in this chapter, including both manual and automatic backup options. Along with optimizing your backup settings, we'll go over some crucial pointers for keeping your Pixel phone up to date with the most recent backups. Whether you're switching to a new Pixel phone or just want to secure your current data, this chapter will provide you with all the information you need to keep your Pixel phone backed up and recover it in case of an emergency.

HOW TO BACK UP AND RESTORE GOOGLE PIXEL ON PC WITH COOLMUSTER ANDROID BACKUP MANAGER

The first way is to use Coolmuster Android Backup Manager, which is very good at backing up and restoring Android phones. With it, you can back up your Google Pixel data on your computer and recover it with just one click, without losing any of the data's quality. And it can open many different types of files, like contacts, texts, call logs, photos, music, videos, documents, and apps. Also, connecting your Google Pixel to this app is easy. You can use a USB cord or a Wi-Fi network, whichever you prefer.

Most importantly, Coolmuster Android Backup Manager's main benefit is that it lets you quickly move data with just one click. The data that you transfer keeps its original file format and quality. Then, before you know how to back up Pixel 2 to a PC and recover Pixel from the backup, you may wonder if such a great tool is compatible with your Google Pixel phone or not.

Well, it works well with all Android phones running Android 4.0 or later. This includes Google Pixel 7/7a/7 Pro/6a/5/4/4 XL/4a/3/3 XL/3a/3a XL/3 Lite/XX/2/2 XL/XL, Google Pixel, and more.

How to back up your Google Pixel to your PC with one click

1. Install Coolmuster Android Backup Manager on your computer and start it up. Then, go to the toolbox and select the Android Backup & Restore section.
2. Use a USB connection to connect your Google Pixel to your computer. Turn on USB debugging and permit your phone when asked. Once this app figures out what device you're using, you'll see the interface below.
3. Back up Google Pixel. On the home page, click the Backup button. Choose the type of info you want to save > Choose a place on your computer to store your information > Below, tap Back Up.

How to quickly restore the Pixel from a backup

Once you've used this app to back up your Google Pixel, you can use it to bring it back at any time.

1. Connect your new Android device to your computer in the same way you did before.

2. Once your computer sees your new Android device, go to the home page and click on the "Restore" button. Choose the phone you want to track from the list > Check the boxes next to the files you want to recover. Click the "Restore" button to bring Pixel back from a backup.

HOW TO USE THE PHONE BACKUP & RESET FEATURE TO BACK UP AND RESTORE YOUR GOOGLE PIXEL

Using Pixel's backup and reset tool is the last way to back up and restore data. To achieve this, you'll need a Google account. Let's look at how to use this method to back up and recover Google Pixel.

How to back up a Google Pixel

1. Go to Settings > Personal > Backup & restart on your Google Pixel phone.

2. Choose Device Backup> Back up to Google Drive. To sign in, you must have a Google account. Then, choose the files on your device that you want to back up. Select pictures backup > Tap Backup & sync if you want to back up your pictures and videos.

How to recover a Google Pixel from a backup

Once a Google Pixel backup is there, you can use this method to bring a Pixel back from a backup. But keep in mind that you can't recover a Google Pixel backup from a phone with a newer version of Android to a phone with an older version of Android.

1. Open the settings menu on your second Pixel phone.

2. Click on User and account > Sign in > Google > Sign in with the same Google account you used for backing up > To recover Pixel from a backup, turn on Automatic restore or follow the steps on the screen.

HOW TO USE THE GOOGLE DRIVE APP TO BACK UP AND RESTORE A GOOGLE PIXEL

In addition to the above professional methods, some online storage services can also back up and recover Google Pixel data, but they have limits on the size of the data they can store and can't back up all Google Pixel data. Here, we'll show you how to use the Google Drive app to back up and recover your Google Pixel.

How to save my Google Pixel XL to my computer as a backup

Install Google Drive from the Google Play Store and open it on your Google Pixel 2.

2. Sign in with a Gmail account, tap the "+" button, and then "Upload." Choose the photos, videos, music, and papers you want.

3. Once you've posted a file, you can check it in Google Drive > My Drive.

How to bring back a Pixel backup from a Google Pixel

When you're done backing up your Google Pixel to Google Drive, you can recover your Pixel from the backup.

1. On your phone, open the Google Drive app and sign in using the same Gmail account.

2. Tap the file you want to recover and hold it down.

3. Press the Download button to bring Pixel back from a file.

CHAPTER ELEVEN

HOW TO SET UP AND USE GOOGLE PIXEL PHONES' PERSONAL SAFETY APP

HOW TO SET UP THE PERSONAL SAFETY APP AND RUNNING

First, you'll want to make sure Google has all the info it needs to help you in a situation.

1. Open the app for Settings.
2. Go to the Safety and Emergency page.
3. Click "Personal Safety."
4. Tap the gear button in the upper left corner of the screen.
5. Here, you can find several choices and features. Let's take them one by one.
6. Emergency SOS is the first. Touch it and choose Set up. Do as you're told.
7. This process will also show you how to set up emergency steps, such as calling emergency services, sharing information with emergency contacts, and recording a video in case of an emergency. If you decide to skip, you can always find these

choices on the main page for setting up safety.
8. Go back to the main choices for safety and tap "Emergency sharing." If you want to share something in case of an emergency, turn it on. This can be a phone call, an emergency call, a low power, or information about where you are right now.
9. Go back to the settings for "Safety" and tap "Crisis alerts." Choose whether or not you want to be notified about neighborhood emergencies and natural disasters.
10. Go back to the setting for safety.
11. If you've already added Emergency contacts, we can move on to the next step. Instead, you should go to Medical Information.
12. Fill out your blood type, your allergies, and the medicines you take. Then tap "More," add any medical notes you want, and tell the app if you're willing to donate an organ or not.
13. Return to the Safety settings page and choose the radio button for Allow access to emergency information.

Turn on the feature.

HOW TO TURN ON THE EMERGENCY SOS NOTIFICATION

1. Press the start button on your Pixel phone five times in a row. This will start a countdown of five seconds.
2. If you accidentally turned on Emergency SOS, you can use the Cancel button to turn it off.
3. If it is an emergency, the phone will continue with the Emergency SOS process and get you help right away.

HOW TO USE THE CAR CRASH DETECTION SYSTEM

Car crash recognition is available on Pixel 3 phones and later, but only in languages and countries where it is turned on. If you know how to use Car crash recognition, the idea is easy to understand. Just go to Safety Settings > Car crash recognition and make sure the feature is turned on. After that, the phone will know if you've been in a car accident on its own. An alarm will go off. You will also be asked to say "Emergency" to call 911 or "cancel" to... stop. You can also use the buttons on the screen to do these things by hand.

If you don't answer within 60 seconds, the system will immediately call 911. It will also tell you about yourself and what might be going on.

CHECK FOR SAFETY AND HOW TO USE IT

You can also use the safety check tool when you think you might be in danger. For example, you can turn it on when you're walking alone, taking the bus, camping, etc. After a certain time, the app will ask you to check-in. If there is no answer, emergency contacts will be told, and emergency sharing will begin.

HOW TO TURN ON SAFETY CHECK

1. Open the app for Settings.
2. Go to the Safety and Emergency page.
3. Click "Personal Safety."
4. Tap the yellow button that says "Safety check" at the bottom of the screen.
5. Choose what you're going to do.
6. Choose how long it will take to do the task.

7. Hit Next.
8. Choose the people you want to take part.
9. Tap the On button.

HOW TO TURN ON IN AN EMERGENCY SHARING

1. Open the app for Settings.
2. Go to the Safety and Emergency page.
3. Click "Personal Safety."
4. Tap the red button that says "Share in an emergency" at the bottom of the screen.
5. Choose the people you want to be a part of it and click "Share."
6. When you turn on Emergency Sharing, your contacts will be able to see where you are and you will have the choice to either Stop or Call 911.

CHAPTER TWELVE

MUSIC

Find what music is being played nearby.

You can ask your Pixel phone to recognize a song so you can discover more about the music you hear around you.

You can view notifications whether your phone is locked or in use, depending on where you wish to receive them.

If your phone is locked, tap the notification twice to get more information about the music. If you're using a phone, press the song notification after expanding the notifications at the top.

HOW TO GET SONG INFO AUTOMATICALLY

1. Open your phone's Settings app.
2. Tap Now Playing, followed by Sound & Vibration.
3. Turn on Identity songs playing nearby.
4. Allow your phone to download the song database for a few minutes.

5. Songs being played nearby will be automatically detected after the download is complete and shown on your lock screen.
6. For more information about a song:
   - Tap the song title if your phone is locked.
   - If you're using a phone, press the song notification after expanding the notifications at the top.

UTILIZE MUSIC SEARCH TO ACCESS ADDITIONAL SONGS.

Many types of music can be recognized by your phone automatically. You can manually search for any tracks that it doesn't have on Google using the music search engine.

1. Open your phone's Settings app.
2. Tap Now playing, followed by Sound & Vibration.
3. Set the lock screen search button to be visible.
4. You can search for music if your phone is unable to recognize it. On your lock screen, select music search to conduct a song search.

FIND THE MUSIC YOU'VE JUST HEARD

1. Open your phone's Settings app.
2. Tap Now Playing, followed by Sound & Vibration.
3. Select Now Playing History.
4. You receive a list of the songs that have been played if you have listened to any of them.
5. Tap the song to share it or to listen to it in a music app.

FAVORITE MUSIC YOU'VE EVER HEARD

Right from your lock screen, you may add a song that is currently playing nearby to your Now Playing favorites list.

On your lock screen, click the music note next to the song's title. The music note is then given a heart. Tap the music note once more to take the song out of your favorites.

To review your preferred music:

1. Launch your phone's Settings application.
2. Tap Now Playing, followed by Sound & Vibration.

3. After selecting Favorites, tap Now Playing History.
4. Tap the red heart icon to remove a song from the favorites list.

MODIFY WHERE NOTIFICATIONS ARE DISPLAYED

You can disable music notifications from appearing at the top of your screen.

1. Launch your phone's Settings application.
2. Toggle between Sound & Vibration, Now Playing, and Notifications.
3. Turn off the notifications for recognized music. Your lock screen still shows song information.

GOOGLE PIXEL'S NOW PLAYING

One of the best features of the Pixel is Now Playing. It uses the same technology as "Hey Google" hot word detection to automatically detect music around you. Since the debut of the Pixel 2, no other phone maker has introduced a rival or substitute for this function. However, using his program Ambient Music Mod, developer Kieron Quinn was able to adapt Now Playing to any unrooted Android 12+ phone.

Shizuku, which can access normally restricted System APIs, makes this possible. Shizuku is used by Ambient Music Mod to access the CAPTURE_AUDIO_HOTWORD API to record audio at predetermined intervals. This audio is afterward processed offline to compare a song's fingerprint to a database that is kept on the device. Similar functionality is provided by Now Playing, however, instead of relying on time intervals, Pixel phones can start and stop music to initiate identification.

For a Pixel-like experience, the Ambient Music Mod resembles Now Playing in appearance. Your lock screen might display the music that is now playing, and upon recognition, a notification may be sent. Even the Now Playing history feature allows you to view all the songs it has identified and favorite them.

This feature operates entirely offline, just like on the Pixel, and no recordings are saved or posted online. Additionally, the software is open source, making it simple to investigate any security or privacy concerns. You don't need to worry about this app any more than you do about any other app, it is safe to state.

The Ambient Music Mod has been tried on OnePlus, Xiaomi, Honor, and Samsung handsets, and it has been successful on each one. Additionally, it is compatible with all SoC vendors and chip speeds. Your phone should be able to run Ambient Music Mod to get Now Playing as long as it runs Android 12.

HOW TO INSTALL AMBIENT MUSIC MOD

It's important to note that steps four through six must be completed each time your phone reboots to activate the Shizuku service.

1. Shizuku can be downloaded and installed from Google Play.
2. Ambient Music Mod can be downloaded and installed from GitHub.
3. Go to the Settings app, enable developer options, and then about the phone. After seven clicks on the build number, enter your pin.
4. To return to the settings main page and select developer options. From there, select developer options and turn on USB and wifi debugging. Network

debugging of wireless devices is permitted.
5. Scroll down in Shizuku once it is open. Under start via wireless debugging, choose pairing. Then select "developer options." For further settings to adjust on Xiaomi, OnePlus/OPPO, or Huawei devices, you must see Shizuku's guide.
6. You ought to be back in developer choices at this point. Select wireless debugging by scrolling down and finding it. Choose a couple of devices with pairing codes when wireless debugging is active. Recall that code, then enter it into the pairing service found a notification from Shizuku and press the send button in your notifications.
7. If everything went smoothly, it would read "pairing successful." If it does, return to the home screen of the Shizuku app and choose Start. Repeat steps 5 and 6 if it doesn't state pairing is successful.
8. Launch the Ambient Music Mod application. To grant Ambient Music Mod access to Shizuku, click get started.

9. Walk through the Ambient Music Mod setup. Choose a country or location that best suits you and the data selections that suit you.
10. Wait for the Now Playing app to download in the setup's Now Playing section, then install it when prompted. Give Ambient Music Mod access to your phone and microphone, and when requested, turn off battery optimizations.
11. Go to the options and advanced tabs in the Ambient Music Mod app. If "Use Alternative Encoding" is checked, Now Play may not function.
12. Return to the app's home page, choose Lock Screen, and turn it on. The current music can be displayed on your lock screen, just like on the Pixel, but you must grant it access to your accessibility settings. Return to Ambient Music Mod when that is enabled and move the location to wherever you want it to be on your lock screen.
13. The Ambient Music Mod ought to be configured.

This feature has been improved with a few changes, albeit at the expense of battery life. You can adjust the recognition interval in settings to reflect how frequently you want it to look for new music. Adaptive recognition is enabled by default, therefore it will wait until the current track has finished playing before checking. Although disabling adaptive recognition might improve recognition, checking more frequently would drain the battery faster. It can also be helpful to catch songs more frequently at the expense of battery life by setting the recognition buffer to five seconds rather than 10.

You should be able to check for app updates and install them directly from within Ambient Music Mod. Weekly updates should be made to the music database, which holds all the songs that Now Playing can recognize. Because Google utilizes the same database for Pixel phones, Ambient Music Mod can identify it if a Pixel can.

CHAPTER THIRTEEN

HOW TO USE GOOGLE PIXEL PHONES' LIVE CAPTION FEATURE

Real-time text transcription of spoken audio is possible using Live Caption. It functions with voice messages, phone calls, podcasts, video calls, and videos. There is more to it than that, though. Because it doesn't require a data or WiFi connection, this function is unique. It works exclusively offline, never stores data, and never leaves your phone.

HOW TO ACTIVATE OR DEACTIVATE LIVE CAPTION

Using the volume controls, enable Live Captioning:

1. Press either the Up or Down button on the hardware.
2. Tap the Live Caption button, which is next to the slider for the volume. It looks like a box for writing.

Use the Settings app to turn on Live Caption:

1. Launch the Settings app.
2. Click on Vibration & Sound.
3. Choose Live Caption.
4. Enable Live Caption

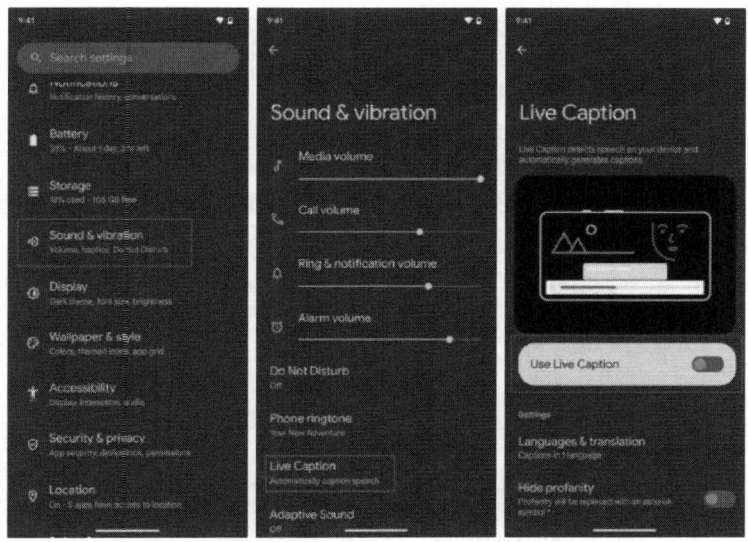

Any audio with speech can now be played, and your device will display a box with live subtitles. The caption box can now be touched and held onto while dragging it up and down the screen to the desired position. The box can be removed by dragging the handle down. By double-tapping the box, you may also make it expand.

HOW TO USE LIVE CAPTION

You can now play any music with speech, and your device will show a box with real-time captions. The caption box can now be moved up and down the screen by tapping and holding it while moving. The box will be gone if you pull it down. You can also double-tap the box to make it bigger.

MANAGING LIVE CAPTION SETTINGS

You can play around with several appealing Live Caption choices to make it more unique for you.

Access the Live Caption Settings:

1. Launch the Settings app.
2. Click on Vibration & Sound.
3. Toggle Live Caption on.

Here, you'll find several possibilities. You can choose whether or not you want to display Live Caption in the volume control, Hide profanity, and Show sound labels. You can also pick when you want Live Caption to start during calls by going into the caption calls menu.

YOU CAN TYPE RESPONSES BY USING A LIVE CAPTION

The Live Caption feature on Pixel 6 and subsequent devices is cool. During calls, you can put in your responses. Your text responses will then be read out to the caller on the other end by the system. The feature must first be activated.

Enable typing responses while on calls:

1. Launch the Settings app.
2. Click on Vibration & Sound.
3. Toggle Live Caption on.
4. Enable typing during calls by switching it on.

You will notice a keyboard icon if this functionality is enabled and you are using Live Caption during a call. Tap it to start typing.

CHAPTER FOURTEEN

GOOGLE ASSISTANT SCREEN CALLS

HOW TO SET UP SCREEN CALLING ON YOUR GOOGLE PIXEL
How to use a Google Pixel to automatically screen calls:

You must configure an automatic Call Screen if you want all incoming calls to be screened. Keep in mind that the feature will only turn on call screening for calls from unknown or private numbers. No contacts of yours will be sent to Call Screen.

1. Ensure that the Phone app is running the most recent version.
2. Open the phone app.
3. Press the menu button with three dots.
4. Enter Settings.
5. Select Call Screen and Spam.
6. Make sure the See Caller and spam ID is turned on.
7. Press Call Screen.

8. Select which incoming callers you want to screen by going to the Unknown call settings.
9. Select the Automatic screen. Under each caller category, reject robocalls.
10. The option to save call screen audio is also available.

After that, Google Assistant will alert you whenever it screens a call. Reading from it will be "Screening an unknown call." You also have the option of answering or declining.

How to use Call Screen Manually

You can choose to manually screen calls if you'd want to be in charge of the call screening process.

1. Get the Phone app open.
2. Press the menu button with three dots.
3. Enter Settings.
4. Choosing Call Screen.
5. To configure it, adhere to the procedures.
6. You should see a screen call option the following time an unknown caller calls you.

7. When prompted, Google Assistant will respond by posing queries. The responses will be live-transcribed for you.
8. You have three options: answer the phone, hang up, or utter some more suggested queries. These recommended inquiries include "Is it urgent?," "Report as spam," "I'll call you back," and "I can't understand."

HOW TO GET THE TRANSCRIPTS OF YOUR SCREENED CALLS OR PRESERVE THE RECORDINGS

Transcripts will be automatically preserved when you use Google Assistant to screen calls. However, you have the option of saving these recordings.

1. Open the phone app.
2. Press the menu button with three dots.
3. Enter Settings.
4. Select Call Screen and Spam.
5. Press Call Screen.
6. Select Save Call Screen audio during setup.
7. Return to the home page of the Phone app.

8. Access the Recents tab.
9. Don't miss the filtered call. The Google Assistant logo will appear next to it.
10. Alternatively, select Transcript with audio.
11. Also available is History, followed by See transcript.

HOW TO MODIFY THE ASSISTANT VOICE FOR SCREENED CALLS

1. Open the phone app.
2. Press the menu button with three dots.
3. Enter Settings.
4. Select Call Screen and Spam.
5. Press Call Screen.
6. Choose Voice.
7. Decide between Voices 1 and 2.

CLEAR CALLING ON PIXEL 7A

The goal of Google's Clear Calling tool is to make calls better for everyone. Clear Calling is powered by Google's AI, which eliminates background noise for both users. Clear Calling differs from other background noise reduction features on other phones since it mutes the other person's voice in addition to any background noise that your Pixel 7a microphone may pick up. When someone makes a call on a busy city street with a Pixel, Clear Calling cancels out the noise in the background for everyone on the call. Being in a crowded or noisy environment doesn't bother me anymore. You can both hear one another. This function is a great way to improve phone calls, and it's a hidden way that Pixel 7 phones stand out from other phones. This function is only available on certain mobile or Wi-Fi connections with a strong enough signal, so it may not always be available.

HOW TO TURN CLEAR CALLING ON OR OFF

Easy steps can be taken to turn on Clear Calling. After you turn it on, you're good to go.

1. Open the Settings app on your Pixel 7a
2. Select Sounds and vibrations.
3. Scroll down and then tap Clear calls.
4. Make Clear Calling available

NOTE

Clear Calling depends on how fast your call is, so it might not work on some calls or in bad weather. Even though the feature requires considerable bandwidth, your Google Pixel phone processes all of the sound data that is used to cancel out background noise. On the Clear Calling support page, you can find out more about how the tool works and what Google's privacy rules are.

CHAPTER FIFTEEN

RECOVER DELETED CONTACTS ON GOOGLE PIXEL

Contacts on my phone frequently get deleted at random, and they also vanish from my Google contacts. "I've had three connections vanish during the past two weeks or so. I can access the text message threads I've had with them, where I'm positive their names were associated when I receive their numbers back. What is happening? Since I switched to Android with my G1 on T-Mobile, this issue has occasionally cropped up.

Contacts abruptly vanished from my Google Pixel? Be more relaxed. On a Google Pixel, deleted contacts can typically be recovered. To learn the hard facts and remedies about Google Pixel Data Recovery, keep reading the sections that follow.

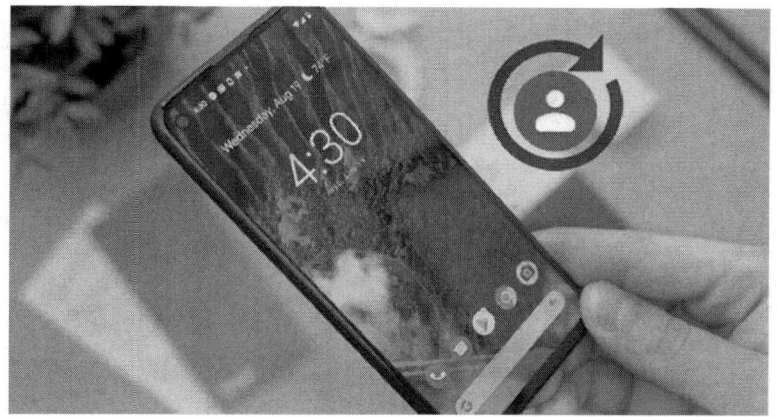

Things to Know Before Recovering Deleted Google Pixel Contacts

What happened to my Google connections, and why? Can lose contacts on a Google Pixel be recovered? You must be curious before moving on to the precise recovery solutions. Your confusion will be resolved in this section.

What Leads Google Pixel Contacts to Disappear?

The following is a list of potential causes for the disappearance of Google Pixel contacts:

- You may have erased certain contacts from your Google Pixel phone intentionally or accidentally.
- Format or factory reset your Google Pixel.

- Several contacts on the target Pixel phone are deleted due to a data migration problem.
- Your Google Pixel sustains physical harm, is cracked, crashes, or experiences ROM flashing.
- Your phone has been infected with malware and a virus, making the data on it unavailable.

Can Delete Contacts from a Google Pixel Be Recovered?

Yes. You have a good possibility of recovering the Google Pixel's deleted contacts. The truth is that even though your Pixel contacts have vanished, they haven't completely vanished from your phone. Instead, they will continue to be present in the device's Unallocated folder until fresh data begins to generate and occupy their space.

Therefore, you must complete the Google Pixel data recovery method before new data overwrites them to effectively recover the deleted contacts.

What to Do Before Google Pixel Data Recovery?

To make it more likely that you can get your info back, you will need to:

- Once the contacts on your Google Pixel have vanished, stop using your phone to prevent any new data from being created.
- Stop any unwanted downloads or updates by immediately turning off the Wi-Fi, mobile data, and internet access.
- The Google Pixel should be turned off before recovery.
- To retrieve the deleted contacts from your Google Pixel, locate a trustworthy data recovery program.

HOW CAN TO RECOVER DELETED CONTACTS WITHOUT BACKUP VIA COOLMUSTER ANDROID SMS + CONTACTS RECOVERY

Coolmuster Android SMS + Contacts Recovery is a small tool that lets you recover your Google contacts even if you don't have a backup. As its name suggests, it is mostly used to recover Android contacts and SMS. You can use it to quickly recover lost contacts from your Google Pixel if you're tired of the complicated features of other apps.

How to use Coolmuster Android SMS + Contacts Recovery to get lost contacts back without a backup?

1. Put the tool on your computer by downloading it.

You'll need to download the app, open it on your PC, and then choose SMS + Contacts Recovery from the app's main screen.

2. Use a USB connection to connect the Google Pixel to the computer.

Use a USB connection to link the Pixel phone to the computer. During the process, you can root your phone if you need to do a deep check. After it is connected, the device info will be shown on the interface.

3. Choose which deleted friends you want to get back on Google Pixel.

Click Contacts in the left window, look at the list of contacts, check the ones you want, and then click the Recover button. The entire process takes under a minute.

HOW TO GET DELETED CONTACTS BACK FROM GOOGLE BACKUP

If you have set up automatic contact sync with your Google account and the backups contain the deleted contacts, you can recover the deleted contacts from the Google backup.

How to Get Deleted Contacts Back from Google Backup

1. Go to the Settings page on your Google Pixel, tap Google, and then tap Set up & Reset.

2. Click the "Restore contacts" button and choose the backup file that has the removed contacts.

3. Click on Restore.

CHAPTER SIXTEEN

DRIVING MODE ON YOUR GOOGLE PIXEL 7A

Driving while using a phone is dangerous. However, a lot of people enjoy using their Android phones to play music or receive notifications while driving. To avoid having to scroll between programs to adjust the music, Driving Mode presents a different user interface than usual, one with larger buttons and several panes. You can increase convenience (or interference, depending on how you look at it) by configuring Drive Control to launch automatically as necessary. You should be able to engage or disable Driving Mode on your Google Pixel phone if you use it throughout your commute.

To use a phone safely while driving:

Set up Do Not Disturb on your phone to prevent interruptions.

Use Android Auto's driving mode if you need to see or interact with your phone while you're driving.

Use the display in your car rather than driving mode if your car has Android Auto built in. Discover Android Auto.

HOW TO SET UP A DRIVING RULE
1. Open the app for setting up your phone.
2. Tap Sound, and then tap Do Not Disturb.
3. Tap Automatically turn on.
4. Tap "Add rule" followed by "Driving."
5. Make sure your rule is turned on at the top.

To delete the rule, tap Delete.

HOW TO ENABLE DO NOT DISTURB ON PIXEL 7A

Do Not Disturb mode is easy to turn on on the Google Pixel 7a, as long as users know how. If someone has moved from iOS to Android or has been using a smartphone that isn't a Pixel, it can take some time to get used to the different menus and settings and to do simple things like turn the phone off or go back to the previous menu. Users won't be able to figure out how to use their phones and all of their features until they use them often. Do Not Disturb mode is one of these features.

Users of the Google Pixel 7a can turn on the "Do Not Disturb" mode in one of two ways. The first and fastest way is to swipe down on the home screen to open the notifications and quick settings section and then tap the Do Not Disturb tile. This will make the phone go silent right away, so calls and alerts won't bother the user. The second way is to use the Settings screen to turn on the "Do Not Disturb" mode. Tap the "Turn on now" button at the top of the screen in Settings > Sound & Vibration > Do Not Disturb. Users can use the "Do Not Disturb" mode when they don't want anything to bother them.

DO NOT DISTURB MODE COULD BE HELPFUL IN MANY SITUATIONS

The Pixel 7a won't buzz or make noise when the Do Not Disturb mode is on. Also, the mode stops the screen from lighting up every time an app sends a message. This is great for when you're in a meeting or a movie theater and don't want to be interrupted, or when you want to spend time with your friends and family without being bothered. Users who don't want to be disturbed but don't want to miss important updates or alerts can add exceptions to the Do Not Disturb mode.

Users can choose what to block and what to show while DND mode is on by going to Settings > Sound & Vibration > Do Not Disturb and choosing from the choices under "What can interrupt Do Not Disturb." The first choice is "People," which lets users allow calls, messages, or notifications from certain contacts. With the 'Apps' option, users can choose which apps can send them alerts. And the "Alarms and other interruptions" setting lets users block or allow alarms, touch sounds, and reminders.

On the Pixel 7a, users can also set a plan instead of turning on Do Not Disturb by hand. Go to Settings > Sound & Vibration > Do Not Disturb and click on 'Schedules.' Some of the things you can schedule are sleeping, an event, while using Driving Mode, and more. Users can set their schedules by hitting "Add more" and filling in the necessary information. With these choices, Pixel 7a users can make exceptions to the DND mode so they don't miss anything important.

CHAPTER SEVENTEEN

HOW TO SET THE PIXEL 7A TO USE 10-BIT COLOR FOR VIDEOS

The number of distinct colors that a camera can render is referred to as bit depth. Most smartphone cameras (and many DSLR cameras) can only render 8-bit color, which means that they can only display 256 shades of each of the three major colors (red, green, and blue) in the spectrum. There are 16.7 million different color tones as a result.

The camera can record 1024 shades of each main hue—1024 shades of red, 1024 shades of blue, and 1024 shades of green—with 10-bit color. There are 1.07 billion different color tones as a result.

The difference between 16.7 million and 1.07 billion is significant, and the result is a video that is crisper, cleaner, and has a much more natural-looking color gamut.

How to make videos on the Pixel 7A use 10-bit color

1. Open the camera application.

Log onto your Pixel 7a Pro and launch the camera app as soon as possible.

2. Change to the video mode

The camera app will be in camera mode when it first launches. To change, tap Video at the bottom.

3. Switch on the 10-bit color

To enable 10-bit color, press the drop-down in the upper left corner. Then, in the popup that appears, tap HDR in the 10-bit HDR item. After doing that, dismiss the settings popup by tapping outside of it.

Now that color shade rendering has significantly improved, you can begin recording videos. Just keep in mind that these files will be bigger than those from 8-bit color films. To free up space on your device, you'll either need to flip back and forth (using 10-bit color for specific videos).

HOW TO UTILIZE THE GOOGLE PIXEL'S MAGIC ERASER

1. Update Google Photos first

The next step is to make sure your Google Photos app is up to date if you own one of the compatible Pixels. Magic Eraser might not show up as a photo-editing tool if that is the case.

2. Choose a photo.

Find the image in Google Photos that you want to edit with Magic Eraser. It should ideally feature distinguishable subjects from a distance as well as up close. Additionally, solid textures are ideal for the editing feature.

3. Use a magic eraser.

After choosing a photo, pick Edit from the bottom menu. If Magic Eraser isn't among the suggested tools, try tapping the Tools category first, then Magic Eraser.

The Pixel will scan the image briefly before highlighting any suggestions for you to delete. From here, you can tap on each subject separately or, if you're feeling very savvy, Erase All. Should you decide not to make the edit, there is an undo toggle at the bottom.

By carefully brushing over the subject, you can also draw attention to the area you want to delete. As long as the shading covers a specific person, place, or object, it doesn't need to be flawless; the Pixel should be able to get information from its surroundings and fill in the space.

Use of camouflage

Those with keen eyes may have discovered the Magic Eraser's Camouflage option. While the procedure for utilizing Camouflage is the same as for using Erase, your Pixel will change the color of the chosen topic to blend in with the surroundings rather than eliminating it from the background. Do you recall the man I described at the beginning of the article who was wearing a bright shirt? That is the purpose of this functionality.

CHAPTER EIGHTEEN

GOOGLE ASSISTANT'S HOLD FOR ME FEATURE

Are you weary of being placed on hold to speak with customer service? Calling businesses or organizations often result in lengthy wait times, but Google Assistant has a handy function that makes speaking with a live person easier.

WHAT IS THE HOLD FOR ME FEATURE IN GOOGLE ASSISTANT, AND HOW DOES IT WORK?

Hold for me is a unique function that waits for you when you are put on hold during any call. This can help when calling companies and other organizations. These can put you on hold for a long time before you can talk to a person.

When you press "Hold for Me," it will wait and let you know when a real person is ready to talk to you. This means you can do something else while you're put on hold.

HOW TO TURN ON THE FUNCTION AND USE IT

You'll need to turn on the tool first.

1. Open the app Phone by Google.
2. Tap the button with three dots.
3. Change the settings.
4. Choose Keep for Me.
5. Toggle on Hold for Me.

DURING A CALL, PUT ME ON HOLD.

You'll have to turn on the tool every time you want to use it.

1. When a call is put on hold, tap Hold for Me.
2. Hit Start.
3. You'll see a message that says "Don't hang up" while you're on hold.
4. When a real person is ready to talk to you, Google Assistant will change the message to "Someone's waiting to talk to you."
5. Choose to call back.

CHAPTER NINETEEN

HOW TO RESET YOUR GOOGLE PIXEL 7A

The Pixel 7a is one of the best phones made by Google in recent years. It brings the speed and quality of Google's A-series phones to a new level. It comes with the most important Android apps and software, and its hardware design is similar to that of its more expensive Pixel brothers. It's important to note, though, that while it's a great phone, it's not perfect, and there may be times when it doesn't work as well as it should.

When I talk about "hiccups," I mean things like apps that crash or software features that stop working for no clear reason.

Most of the time, resetting an Android device makes it work like it's brand new again. This is because it gets rid of user-installed apps and other files that can sometimes slow it down. There are also times when an app crashes, freezes, or something else goes wrong and your phone just needs a quick reboot. Having said that, there are two ways to restart an Android phone:

Restart/Reboot: This is also called a "soft reset," and all it does is turn your phone off and on again. This gives it a chance to fix any unexpected problems with how it works.

Reset: This method, which is also called a "hard reset" or "factory reset," deletes everything saved on your phone, such as your apps, settings, files, photos, and songs. It is recommended that you back up your files on your PC or online using cloud storage systems.

If your Pixel 7a isn't working right or you want to reset it to factory settings so you can sell it or give it to someone else, try one of the ways below:

BASIC RESTART

1. Press the power button down for a few seconds.
2. Your screen should show you a menu with choices like "Emergency," "Lockdown," "Power Off," and "Restart."
3. Choose "Restart."
4. Then, your phone should turn off and then turn back on by itself in a few seconds.

FACTORY RESET

Factory restarting your phone deletes all of your personal information, so it's best to back up your files on a PC or in the cloud.

1. Open your "Settings" app.
2. Go to "System" and then "Reset Options."
3. Tap "Erase All Data (Factory Reset)"
4. Tap on "Erase all Data."
5. Then, your phone should delete your information and restart itself after a few minutes.

FORCE RESTART

If your phone won't work and you can't get to the settings choices through the screen, you might need to force restart it.

Hold down the power button for a few seconds until the screen turns off. After that, it should come back on by itself.

TWENTY

TIPS AND TRICKS

OPEN THE CAMERA QUICKLY

If you've ever missed a great photo opportunity because it took too long to open your phone and find the camera app, this tip is for you.

If you double-press the power/lock button on your phone, the camera will open if a setting on your phone is turned on. Whether you're on the lock screen or in an app, the camera will take over right away to give you those extra few seconds you need to quickly take a picture or start recording.

Go to Settings > System > Gestures > On to turn this on. Open the camera quickly.

GET TO GOOGLE PAY QUICKLY FROM THE LOCK SCREEN

Once you've set up Google Pay for mobile payments, you can use it right from the lock screen. When your phone is locked, a small card picture will show up at the bottom right of the screen. When you tap it, GPay opens quickly so you can use it to pay for things.

If it's not there, make sure Google Pay is set up for the card you want to use, and then go to Settings > Display > Lock Screen and make sure the 'Show Wallet' button is turned on.

MULTILINGUAL KEYBOARD

If you know more than one language and use both often, you might find a bilingual or multilingual keyboard helpful. rather than having to move between languages all the time.

Tap "Gboard" after going to Settings > System > Languages > On-screen keyboard. Now tap "languages" and "add a keyboard." Choose one of the languages from the list.

When you start typing now, the installed keyboard will automatically know if you're writing in English or Spanish, and it can fix and suggest spellings for both languages without you having to switch.

TURN ON THE QUICK TAP

Here's what you need to do to turn on Quick Tap:

1. Open the menu for settings.
2. Go to the topic for System.
3. Select Gestures.
4. Choose Tap Quick.
5. Select your order.

CHANGE THE SIZE OF THE KEYBOARD

All you have to do to make up for the gap is move the keyboard up. This should make it easy to type and give you a better view of the bottom row of keys. Here's how to change the settings on your keyboard:

1. Open the menu for settings.
2. Tap where it says "Search" and type "keyboard."
3. Find the answer for "Keyboard height" and tap on it.

You can choose from seven button heights on Google.

SIGN UP TWICE WITH YOUR FINGERS

Here's what you need to do:

1. Try going to Settings.
2. Move your cursor to Fingerprint Unlock.

3. When asked, enter your PIN.
4. Choose to add your fingerprint.
5. By following the steps, your whole fingerprint will be scanned.
6. From the same menu, you can also remove fingerprints you don't want.

TURN OFF YOUR MIC OR CAMERA QUICKLY

This one is very short, but it's a brand-new feature. The camera and mic can be turned on and off by pulling down the settings shade. If you tap on one, your camera and mic will be blocked right away, so no app on your phone can use them.

ADD A RAW SWITCH TO THE CAMERA

You can have a switch that lets you choose between RAW and JPE if you want to. Open your camera, tap the settings cog in the corner, and then tap more settings'. Now, click on "Advanced" and turn on the "RAW+JPEG control" choice.

When you open the camera settings screen that shows up over the viewfinder or monitor, you'll now see a switch that lets you choose between shooting in RAW+JPEG or just JPEG.

STOP USING THE GOOGLE DISCOVER PAGE

You can turn off the Google feed page, which is usually on the left side of the home screen and shows you news and videos that Google thinks are important to you. Just hold down on your wallpaper for a few seconds and choose "Home setting." Now, turn off the option that says "Swipe to access the Google app."

AUTOMATICALLY FIND SONGS

This Google Pixel trick lets you hear what song is playing close without opening an app or even unlocking your phone. Even if you don't use Shazam, it's like having it on your lock screen forever.

This tool is cool because it works even when you don't have a data connection. Nothing is ever sent to Google, and you can use it even when you don't have a data connection. From the settings, you can also get a full list of all the songs it knows. You can even put a link to this list on your home screen so you can always get to it quickly.

You can turn this on by going to Settings > Sound & Vibration> Now Playing (or, in some versions, Settings > Sound > Now Playing). Songs are shown both on the lock screen and in the pull-down menu for notifications.

CONCLUSION

The Pixel 7a is the best Android phone in the middle price band. It fits even more of the features of a high-end smartphone into a smaller, less expensive model.

Google's phone is faster than most of its competitors because it has the best chip, a lot of RAM, and a good amount of storage. It has a great, bright screen with a 90Hz refresh rate, which is a key feature of high-end phones along with wireless charging.

With good software and five years of support, you can use it for a longer time. The camera is the best in its class, it beats the cameras on many phones that cost twice as much and completely blows away the competition in the mid-range.

The back is not glass, but most people will still put it in a case. The battery lasts for 34 hours, which is good enough for a good day but not the best.

INDEX

BACK UP YOUR GOOGLE PIXEL PHONE AND RESTORE IT, 121
BASIC SETTINGS TO CHANGE AS SOON AS YOU UNBOX YOUR NEW PIXEL 7A, 65
CAMERA, 85
CONCLUSION, 179
DIFFERENCE BETWEEN THE GOOGLE PIXEL 7 PRO, PIXEL 7, AND PIXEL 7A, 35
DRIVING MODE ON YOUR GOOGLE PIXEL 7A, 158
FEATURES OF GOOGLE PIXEL 7A, 18
GET TO KNOW YOUR GOOGLE PIXEL 7A, 14
GOOGLE ASSISTANT SCREEN CALLS, 146
GOOGLE ASSISTANT'S HOLD FOR ME FEATURE, 167
HOW TO ACTIVATE OR DEACTIVATE LIVE CAPTION, 142
HOW TO ENABLE DO NOT DISTURB ON PIXEL 7A, 159
HOW TO GET SONG INFO AUTOMATICALLY, 133
HOW TO RESET YOUR GOOGLE PIXEL 7A, 169
HOW TO SET THE PIXEL 7A TO USE 10-BIT COLOR FOR VIDEOS, 163
HOW TO SET UP A DRIVING RULE, 159

HOW TO SET UP AND USE GOOGLE PIXEL PHONES' PERSONAL SAFETY APP, 128
HOW TO SET UP THE GOOGLE PIXEL 7A FACE UNLOCK, 58
HOW TO SET UP YOUR GOOGLE PIXEL 7A, 55
HOW TO TURN ON THE PIXEL 7A 90HZ SCREEN, 63
HOW TO USE GOOGLE PIXEL PHONES' LIVE CAPTION FEATURE, 142
HOW TO UTILIZE THE GOOGLE PIXEL'S MAGIC ERASER, 164
INTRODUCTION, 13
MESSAGES, 99
MUSIC, 133
OPEN THE CAMERA QUICKLY, 173
PHOTOS, 106
RECOVER DELETED CONTACTS ON GOOGLE PIXEL, 152
SPECIFICATIONS FOR THE GOOGLE PIXEL 7A, 16
TRANSFER OF DATA, 112
UTILIZE MUSIC SEARCH TO ACCESS ADDITIONAL SONGS., 134

Printed in Great Britain
by Amazon